Willie's Tales & Travels

Willie's Tales & Travels

Willie Smith

Willie Smith

The Shetland Times
Lerwick
2011

Willie's Tales & Travels

First published by The Shetland Times Ltd., 2011.

Copyright © Willie Smith, 2011.

ISBN 978-1-904746-68-3

Front cover photo: Twisting roads in Faroe.

Back cover photo: The author with his grandson, Jamie.

All rights reserved.
No part of this publication may be reproduced, stored in a retrieval system, or transmitted, in any form, or by any means, electronic, mechanical, photocopying, recording or otherwise, without the prior written permission of the publishers.

Willie Smith has asserted his rights under the Copyright, Designs and Patents Act, 1988, to be identified as the author of this work.

British Library Cataloguing-in-Publication Data
A catalogue record for this book is available from the British Library

Printed and published by
The Shetland Times Ltd.,
Gremista, Lerwick,
Shetland, Scotland. ZE1 0PX

CONTENTS

Acknowledgements	vii
Peerie Meggie	1
Brucie	5
The Hand Grenade	10
The Clerk of Works	12
Pee	15
The Manager Inspects	17
The Flying Farmer	21
The Vanishing Cod	32
Peerie Charlie's Peats	37
Holiday Visit	39
The Viewing	41
Regatta Times	43
The Deep Dive	56
Chief Abadou	58
Regatta Music	63
Da Stuart Turner	72
The Lino Affair	80
Assassination Attempt	84
Robbie Da Diver	86
The Gutting Machine	88
Da Rundstykke Affair	93
The Old Smiddy	98
Water Connecting	102
The Night My Father Died	107
A Story From 1920	112
More on Da Privy	118
Mal De Mer (Spewing)	122
Bertie and Willie on Dalsnibba	130
Mortar Shells	136
The Swedish Connection	139
303 Rifle Cartridges	159
Replenish at Vee Skerries	161
The Anonymous Letter	167
Around Scalloway	171
Wells Around Scalloway	258
Skirts	260
Lost	261
Glen	262
The Black Belt	267
Scalloway Servicemen and women	271

ACKNOWLEDGEMENTS

ONCE AGAIN I am indebted to my son, William C. T. Smith BSc, for the time he has spent correcting my English. My thanks also to friends past and present with whom I have shared yarns over the years, especially Jim Smith OBE of Berry Farm.

For photos my thanks go to Jim Smith, Stella Ward, Keith and Joyce Pottinger, Willis Duncan, Muriel Cheyne, Kris Calder, William C. T. Smith and Capt. Billy Duncan.

Most of the photos in this book were taken by Clement J. Williamson.

PEERIE MEGGIE

AT THE WEST END of Scalloway's Main Street was the premises of Nicolson & Co., grocers, coal merchants, purveyors of ropes and twines, paints, and everything else you could think of. They had many stores and sheds, including the Netloft – later to become Norway House – which was built around 1920 by my father and Uncle Robbie. It was called the Netloft as that was its primary use, although on the ground floor was a sawmill with a lot of wood stored in racks, which was later to become a coal shed. At the very top of the building, herring nets were stored all winter and the first floor was where the nets were mended. On three sides of the building was a balcony over which nets were hung to dry. A lot of women were employed on the first floor mending the herring nets; they had an overseer who did not allow any speaking. My sister Chrissie worked there for a time. She also occasionally got nets from a cousin in Burra Isle to mend in our house and I, too, learned to mend and would often help her. To me at a young age it was more like fun than work.

Da 'birdie window' with Nicolson & Co. shop, on right. Photo: Willie Smith

Willie's Tales & Travels

Across the road from Nicolson & Co. was a large stone-built building. At the Main Street end, on the first floor, Bobby Nicolson had a dental surgery. The big window that looked on to Main Street was called the 'birdie window', as Bobby kept a lot of canaries and budgies there. The birdie window was a great attraction and there were always bairns and grown-ups standing looking in. On the ground floor, underneath the surgery, was my father's joinery workshop. To the seaward side of the workshop stayed Bob Yonson and his wife, Ruby. When they moved to the West Shore bungalow their rooms became the offices of the Shetland Bus. On the Netloft side, opposite Bob Yonson lived Maggie Tulloch, who was better known as Peerie Meggie. Seaward from Peerie Meggie lived Davie Mackenzie – a fish-curer – and his wife. Seaward again was another coal shed, which after the war became the 'Hush Hush Plant', where machinery ran day and night and operatives worked in shifts around the clock. Rumour had it that this secretive facility was producing heavy water.

As far as I remember, Peerie Meggie had just one room with a closet store of some kind. My brother Tammie once went to

Maggie B. Watt, Willa Ratter, Baba Umphray and Davie McKenzie, 1935.
Courtesy Muriel Cheyne

Peerie Meggie

whitewash her ceiling and when it came time to have a cup of tea she hurried up to Nicolson & Co.'s shop. When my sister Chrissie came to serve her, Meggie leaned across the counter and whispered confidentially, "Twa fancies for him."

The phrase "Twa fancies for him" was a byword used for a long time after.

When the Royal Artillery battery was being constructed at Port Arthur, all the surrounding area was enclosed with fences and barbed wire. The flat area (opposite the marina) where the Boating Club and boats now stand was also closed in, right up to Robbie Rolly where the guard hut was sited. One day a coal steamer berthed at Blacksness Pier and soon lorries started to ferry the coal to this flat piece of ground. Lorries in those days were few and far between so they were a great attraction to small boys; if you could get a driver to take you for a run to Blacksness and back then that just made your day. I recall getting runs with Jimmy Hall, and sometimes on Nicolson & Co.'s lorry with Jimmy Smith.

The road going past Nicolson's shop and opposite Peerie Meggie's door had a slight camber, so if the not very large lorries were fully loaded some coal would fall onto the road. One day, watching a lorry going past, I saw Peerie Meggie run from her door carrying a basin. She gathered up the pieces of coal that had fallen then hurried back into her house. This amused me, so I waited for the next lorry, the same thing happened and Meggie got a few more pieces of coal. Another lorry must have had its coal unevenly loaded as, when it passed by, about half a hundredweight or more of coal fell off outside Peerie Meggie's door! This time I helped Meggie fill her basin. "There's plenty coal here for everybody," she said, so I ran to our house for a bucket.

After a few more lorries had gone past my bucket was full, and coal was piling up in Meggie's lobby. I thought I was doing something great for the war effort, and for our house – we had a Number 7 stove and it always needed coal. I proudly made my way up the brae to the house but when I came in, carrying the full bucket, I was asked, "What's that? Where did you get that coal?"

My reply was the same phrase now heard many times in police stations and law courts, "It fell off the back of a lorry."

"Well," I was told, "go and put it back where you found it." Feeling very hard done by, I went back down the brae with the bucket of coal. Peerie Meggie was still there with her basin.

"Meggie," I asked, "do you want this coal, as wir folk said I was to put it back."

"Yes, yes, my dear. Put it in the lobby."

Peerie Meggie was the only one who benefited from the coal that fell off the lorries. The coal was locally known as 'service coal' as it was for servicemen at Port Arthur, Houll Road, Meadowfield Road, Berry Camp and Castle Camp. However, the coal was very poor quality; it was actually 'surface coal', and had been misheard by someone as service coal. Peerie Meggie did not care whether it was service or surface, to her it was free and it kept her fire burning for a long time.

BRUCIE

IN THE WINTER of 1957-58, while working in Burravoe, Yell, I became acquainted with Brucie and Kate Henderson. We became good friends and I always looked forward to visiting them at their home in Arisdale. A visit to Brucie and Kate often started with a run from Burravoe on the back of Magnie Mann's motorbike. We would then sit listening to Brucie's tales – prompted by Magnie's "Brucie, tell him about..." – accompanied by the hissing of the Tilley lamp. The stories were suspended frequently for tea and Kate's bannocks, before they were recommenced with renewed vigour. Coming out into a fine frosty night, with a myriad of stars twinkling and not a light to be seen, you could not help but take a peek back over your shoulder while walking to the main road; you never could be sure what might be lurking in the valley of Arisdale.

The first time I met Brucie was at the Burravoe Hall, where I was working with my brother's firm of T. Smith & Son, doing alterations.

Brucie and the author. Photo: John Leask

One of the men came one day and said that Brucie Henderson had arrived and would like to speak with me. I had heard of Brucie, but this was to be the first time I would see him. My first impression was of a tall, gaunt man with a flat cap, a long black coat and, about his neck, a thick woollen scarf.

He greeted me with, "Are ye Mister Smith?" I said I was, and he continued, "I'm Brucie Henderson fae Arisdale, and I have a drawing window Blind Peter made for me. I would like ye to come and put her in da sooth end of Arisdale."

After consulting with the boss in Scalloway, I was to go and have a look at the window and where it was to go. So one afternoon, John R. Tulloch and I set off for Arisdale on J.R.'s motorbike. I was curious to see this drawing window made by partially sighted Blind Peter. J.R. and I sat and talked with Brucie and Kate (who came from South Whiteness) for a while then were taken to see the window and where it was to go. It had been made by Peter Tulloch, who was born in South Yell, in 1895, and had lost most of his sight when a child. I was told by his neighbour, Thomas John Robertson, that Peter could see out of the corners of his eyes and enjoyed woodworking, making tables, chairs and even cartwheels. I remember meeting Peter at the Ulsta shop in 1957. I had served my time as a joiner and made many sash and case (drawing) windows, so I was most impressed with the window considering Peter's sight problems.

We measured up the job for the materials required and it was agreed that J.R. and Hunter Sandison would do the work. Once the materials had been gathered together for the installing of the window, an afternoon visit by tractor to Arisdale was arranged. Magnie Anderson from Ulsta drove the tractor, with Hunter, James Sinclair, and myself aboard the trailer. It was a fine frosty afternoon with a smattering of snow at the edges of the road. We enjoyed the run in the crisp air until we were about two-thirds up the Arisdale road, where the trailer bogged in up to the axle. We then had to carry the materials the rest of the way to the house. By this time it had started to snow in earnest and it was getting quite dark. Once all the materials had been carried to the house and stowed away, we were about to set off back to Burravoe, when Brucie said, "You

Hunter, J. R., Jamie, the author. Photo: Willie Smith

will do no such thing. Kate has made tea so in you come." That was an order.

Kate was baking bannocks and frying bacon and eggs, the Tilley lamp was making a pleasant hissing sound, and the room was filled with peat reek from the Truburn. There was so much reek and styooch you could hardly see Kate across the room. It was all most splendid after the cold air outside. The meal we had that night at Arisdale was superb and could not have been equalled by any top restaurant.

When we had finished eating and were leaning back in our chairs, Magnie said, "Well boys, if you want me to put you back to Burravoe we will have to leave now as I have animals to feed and attend to." We told him just to go, as because there was no wind we would walk to Burravoe. But when Magnie had left, Brucie said, "Nobody walks to Burravoe with this night of snow," and he phoned Bobby Hugh Williamson from Burravoe to come and fetch us. Later, after thanking Kate for the meal, we left and walked to the road where the car met us.

A few weeks later the window was installed and Brucie and Kate were pleased as they could now see the main road.

Willie's Tales & Travels

Brucie and Kate with Blind Peter's window. Photo: Willie Smith

John Leask, Brucie and Harold Hunter at plane crash site. Photo: Willie Smith

Brucie

Summer invitations to Arisdale were always on a Sunday afternoon. On one occasion Brucie told me he would take us for a walk in the hills of Arisdale to where a plane had crashed during the war. On this visit were Harold Hunter, John Leask, a telecoms engineer, and myself. Brucie delighted us with many tales all the way to the wreck of the plane, and then many more at the site. At the house, Kate had tea waiting and made us very welcome.

Brucie and Kate were very kindly people, and Brucie was quite a character. I'm very glad to be able to say, "Oh yes, I knew Brucie from Arisdale."

THE HAND GRENADE

ONE DAY, many years ago, I thought I would clear a corner of the shed. Bruck had been building up there for quite a while and a council skip had providentially appeared nearby. I wondered what could be in the cardboard box I held. Was it some long lost item, or just more bruck? Indeed, the box was full of bruck, but my eyes fell on a strange object lying in the corner. Could it really be a hand grenade? Yes, it was a hand grenade from the wartime. It looked like the real thing, with a pin, which when pulled released the plunger which would have set the fuse going. There was no fuse, however, and nothing to explode; it was a dud, a dummy, a practise grenade. It reminded, though, of where it had come from.

The year was 1945. The war had ended, and all around Scalloway were army huts with all kinds of equipment left behind. Among all this junk, one of my workmates had found this very same hand grenade. How he found out it was a dud, I don't know. Perhaps it was passed it around in a game of Russian Roulette! Anyhow, much fun was had with it, which today would be very much frowned on and likely result in prosecutions.

Four of my workmates were preparing an area for an extension on a building; there were no diggers or JCBs in those days, just men with picks and shovels. One of the men had just returned home from the forces, two were young teenagers, and the fourth was a good bit older. One day the three younger men returned early after lunch and decided to play a prank on their older fellow worker, who did not know of the existence of the hand grenade. In the corner where he had been digging, they laid the hand grenade down, covered it with a little earth and then moved away. Soon he appeared, and when he started digging with his shovel he heard the clink of metal on metal. The others watched keenly as he scraped with his shovel and the hand grenade rolled clear. He moved smartly away and shouted for them to come quickly and see what he had dug up. They hurried over and the ex-army man said, "Oh my, a hand grenade. I've worked with them." He picked it up and said, "If you pull this

The Hand Grenade

pin out it will set the fuse going," and promptly pulled the pin. The plunger went down with a loud snap, and the old fellow raced away as fast as his legs could carry him, as his workmates roared with laughter. Realising he had been had, he raced back, picked up his shovel, and the three had to run for their lives. It was quite some time before friendly relations were restored.

THE CLERK OF WORKS

IN THE LATE 1940s, the government of the day decided to build extra classrooms at some rural schools. The building designed had two classrooms – one for technical subjects and one for English – plus a cloakroom and the usual toilets. There was also a boiler room, and the building had radiators heated by a coke burning boiler. One such building was built at the Scalloway school where it served well. I don't remember what the building design was called but its initials were H.O.R.S.A. and it was referred to as the Da HORSA building

The building firm I worked for was awarded the contract to construct the Scalloway HORSA. All the materials for the building were supplied except the concrete blocks, glass, shingle, sand and cement. There was even a clerk of works to direct operations. The main structure had reinforced concrete pillars set in concrete and bolted to reinforced concrete rafters, which in turn were bolted together at the ridge. It sounds very simple when you talk about it. However, to get them lined up and to stay up while you got the concrete around the feet of the pillars could be a bit tricky. In those far off days there were no scaffolding poles, and no kind of builder's helps. All we had were lengths of four by two, battens, sarking boards and trestles. To get the pillars and concrete rafters in place and bolted together took half dozen men and lots of ingenuity. The pillars had to be spaced evenly and accurately, for the windows had to fit between the openings. They had to be plumb both ways, and the rafters had to be in line and well supported, as they were quite heavy.

We first made the base of the building. It was measured-off, then built using concrete blocks and with a concrete floor, with holes left for the pillars. Once this was done – with directions from the clerk of works – and the concrete was set and hard, the work began to erect the pillars. Three sets were erected at a time as that took up all the trestles and supports we had at our disposal. As I said, it was tricky work getting everything lined up and supported and the feet of the pillars set the correct distance down in the holes. Double wedges were in place at the foot of the supports and it looked like we had done a good job, with the pillars and rafters set to a quarter of an inch. The next job was to mix concrete to pour in the holes around the feet of the pillars. Soon that was done and everyone was feeling very relieved that we had managed so well with what had looked like a daunting task. There were quite a few more to be done, but the general feeling now was that the others would be easier as we would follow the same procedure.

The clerk of works seemed relieved too and said very cheerfully, "That's splendid now. Is all the concrete in place?"

We were all standing amid the supports and trestles, and someone said that yes, the concrete was indeed all in place. At this, and without any warning, the clerk of works grabbed a hammer and knocked away one of the main supports. There was a rumble as it came adrift and then a crash as the other supports started to move, as well as the pillars and rafters. By this time we were all – including the clerk of works – making a very quick exit. The rafters were broken where they had joined the now leaning pillars, which were also broken at the top and bottom. In silence we surveyed the scene which looked like a war-time bomb site.

Then the silence was broken. John, one of the men, addressed the clerk of works and gave him surely the worst telling-off he had ever had in his life, and included many words which I cannot repeat. He asked some very pertinent questions concerning his capability, and called him the world's biggest idiot. John concluded with saying that surely everyone knew that concrete would have had to set before you could take the supports away.

Then the foreman said, "Jamie, run to the workshop and tell the boss to come here as quick as he can."

Soon the boss arrived, already knowing the whole story from Jamie. He looked at the devastation in silence, then shook his head and said to the clerk of works, "And what are you going to do about this?"

A very discomfited clerk of works said, "I will phone the department tonight and report it as storm damage. They will send replacement pillars and rafters and I will sign a form to send, so that you will get paid for all the extra work involved." Turning to the now highly amused workmen, he said, "I am truly sorry."

He was duly forgiven but, for the duration of the job, everyone kept an eye on him at all times, just in case!

PEE

School and schoolhouse. Photo: Clement J. Williamson

IN MY SCHOOLDAYS the toilets and play-sheds at the Scalloway School were very primitive by today's standards. The toilets were outside and separated from the play area by a partition, and had a door that could be keyed. In the toilet area was a urinal and four compartments with toilet pans.

The exterior door was a lining door with three bars across, and had suffered abuse over the years. The lock had at one time been below the middle bar, but had been replaced a few times and was now in a new position above the middle bar. This door was only closed and keyed at weekends and holidays.

One playtime I went to the toilet only to find the door closed and a lot of boys gathered outside. "What's happened?" I asked.

"Some boys are inside and holding the door shut," I was told, "and we can't get in to pee." We pushed on the door but could not move it. Soon the bell would ring to resume classes and then what would we do?

It was suggested that someone should pee in through the disused keyhole. We all agreed that this was a good idea. But who would do the deed? A young boy, who was cross-legged and just bursting, said he would do it and, stepping up to the door, he pulled up the leg of his short trousers (we all wore short trousers then) and held his appendage to the disused keyhole.

With the pressure that had built up inside him it was a good strong stream of urine that shot through the keyhole. He then quickly stepped back as, suddenly, the door opened to reveal his older brother! The side of his short trousers was soaking wet and a stream of hot liquid was running down his bare leg into his sock. We all howled with laughter, then rushed through the now open door to do our business.

THE MANAGER INSPECTS

WILLIAM RAE DUNCAN was a big man; tall, powerful and well built. In the 1930s he was manager of Hay & Co.'s shop and premises at Blacksness. Part of his job as manager was to inspect Blackness Pier, although why, I do not know. It was decided that the face of the stone-built pier, both above and below water, should be looked at to check the condition of the stones. Of course, the person undertaking this job would have to don a diving suit and walk along the seabed. This really should have been a job for a professional diver but the task fell to William Rae Duncan.

A diver at Blacksness, Peter Slater holding helmet. Photo: Clement J. Williamson

Willie's Tales & Travels

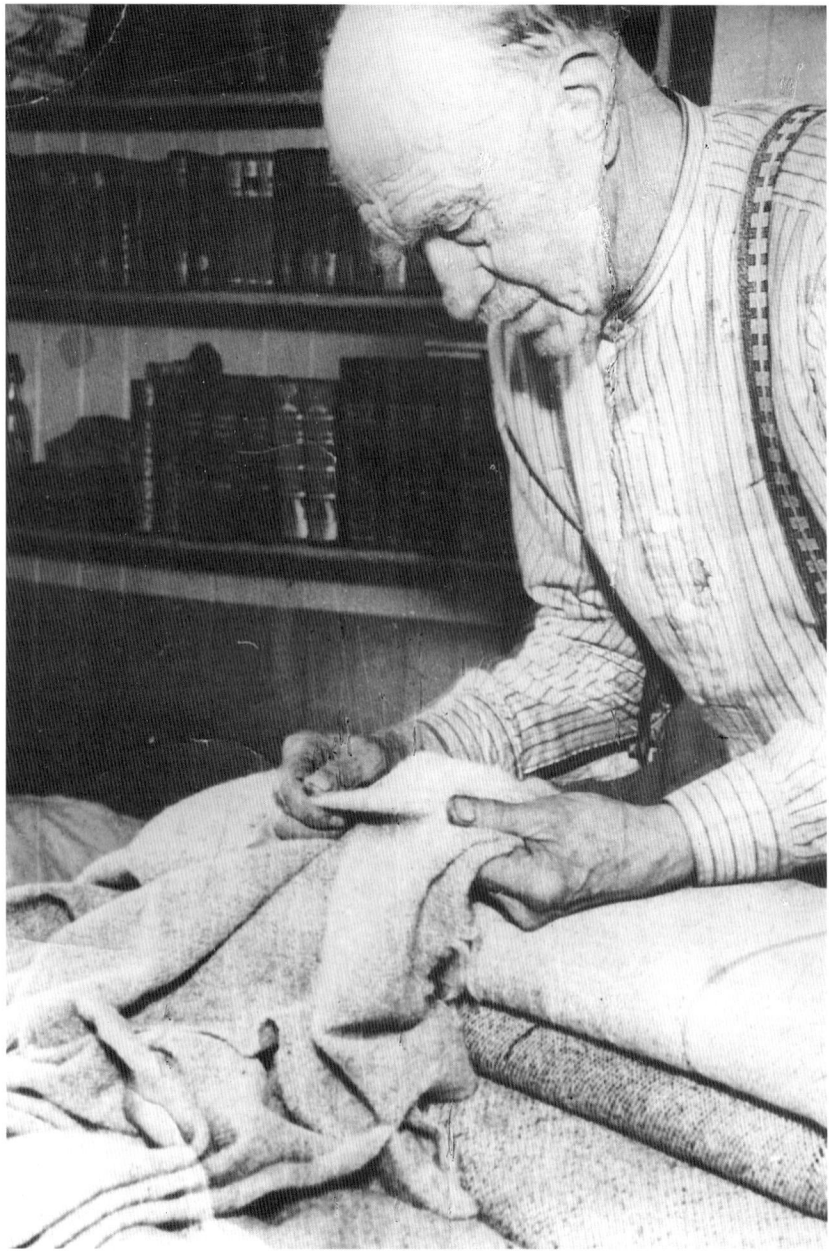

Rae Duncan checks over tweed. Photo: Clement J. Williamson

The Manager Inspects

So, a diving suit and all the associated gear was procured, and local employees of Hay & Co. who operated the diving equipment set the operation in motion. Rae Duncan, as he was known locally, was a bit apprehensive about the inspection but there was no way he could get out of it. To get a big man like him into a diving suit for the first time was quite an undertaking. All the weights and belts and great heavy boots must have felt like a ton.

When everything was in place and the helmet on, Rae Duncan was helped to the ladder at the side of the pier. Climbing slowly onto it, and before the faceplate was screwed in place, he said to the two men who were now starting to pump the air, "Remember now, boys, whatever you do give me plenty of air."

The man holding the safety rope and air hose screwed the faceplate on then gave Rae Duncan a pat on the helmet, the signal to start down the ladder. He reached the bottom safely and soon could be seen walking along the seabed, so everything seemed to be alright.

The two men manning the pump were turning the handles at the usual pace. Then one of them said, "Man, I have just been thinking, Rae Duncan is a big man and he might need more air than you or I would. Maybe we should give him a bit more."

His companion agreed, so they doubled the speed on the handles. They pumped away vigorously for a few minutes then, without any warning, Rae Duncan exploded out of the sea with an almighty splash and lay floating on the surface, his suit blown up like a balloon!

Apparently, no one had told him how to adjust the air valve on the helmet and the extra air the men had so thoughtfully given him had been unable to escape. The man holding the safety rope had to pull him in to the ladder and release some of the air before helping him onto the pier.

It was a frightening experience and there would be no more managerial inspections of the pier.

During the latter years of his life, William Rae Duncan carried on a successful weaving business in the ground floor of his house at New Road, and later (when I remember him) in a shed near the High Road, or Castle Street as it is today. Rae Duncan was an excellent fiddler and much in demand at functions in the public hall. A man of much reading and learning, he was entirely self taught and had, I have been told, a good knowledge of the Greek language. A visiting journalist called Hugh Morton dubbed him the 'Scholar Weaver'.

THE FLYING FARMER

WHEN Jim Smith from Berry Farm was demobbed from the Royal Air Force he thought he would like to build the small speedboat he had acquired plans for while serving in Singapore. Times were hard and it was difficult to find any suitable wood but 'where there's a will there's a way' and Jim found enough to make a start.

He worked at the boat in his spare time from the farm work, occasionally getting more wood until eventually the boat was completed and launched. In Jim's own words, "She floated."

He had a Morris engine, which he fitted in the boat, but alas, as a speedboat, that was not a success so when someone offered him, for a fiver, an Austin 7 car engine which was light and reliable, he accepted.

The engine needed a new manifold so Jim decided to make a mould and cast the manifold out of aluminium. At the farm they had a small portable forge, used in the shoeing of horses. Jim thought this would maybe be suitable enough to melt the scrap aluminium for the casting, which could be a dangerous and risky business. He next had to get a pot thick enough to withstand the heat and melt the aluminium without melting itself. He found a pot at the farm, but it melted and molten metal ran into the air pipe of the forge, which then had to be drilled out.

At that time, the village dump was at the foot of the Scord. Jim got some young boys, who were always at the farm, to go and look for cast iron pots. At last one was found which seemed thicker and heavier than the others and it worked fine. So, the time was ready for the casting to be done; the forge was well alight, the scrap aluminium to hand, and the usual audience of small people were kept well back out of harm's way.

As the aluminium melted a lot of heat was generated. With Jim being so close to the forge the plastic belt holding up his trousers also melted and, much to the amusement of his young audience, his trousers dropped to the floor! The casting continued with his trousers held up by piece of string.

Jim in Jinta. Photo: Clement J. Williamson. Courtesy Jim Smith

The new manifold, when finished, fitted well to the Austin 7 engine. Jim worked on the engine to convert it to a marine engine and, when fitted in the boat, it was a great success. The boat now had a good turn of speed and the engine was far more powerful than he had expected. A new sport was now to be seen in Scalloway – water skiing. On fine Sunday afternoons there was always a crowd at the Bool Green watching the more daring try this new sport, with always a laugh to be had at the tumbles and splashes.

Jim had always had a dream that he would at some time like to build an aeroplane. Now, having seen the power that the Austin 7 engine could produce in the boat, he wondered if it could fly a light plane. He improved on the engine by discarding bits and pieces which would not be required on a plane – such as the flywheel and timing wheels – and altered the magneto and other parts to make the engine lighter. He then found some suitable pieces of wood and fashioned a propeller. The propeller would have to be tested and Jim decided this would have to be done scientifically. He built a track on the workbench, on which was mounted the engine so that it could move easily.

Someone had previously given Jim a correspondence course on aerodynamics and all the basics of aeroplanes, such as thrust, centres of gravity, lift and so on. Bearing all this in mind, plus his pilot training in the RAF, he attached a spring balance to the rear of the engine so the pounds thrust could be measured. When he started the engine the suction from the propeller lifted the wood shavings and sawdust from the floor and whirled it all around the

Jim and his first plane. Photo: Willie Smith

Willie's Tales & Travels

Jim with his first plane. Photo: Willie Smith

workshop. Jim said it was like a thunderstorm. Luckily, the engine stopped. He then made different propellers and the pounds thrust gradually improved. With one particular propeller he wondered about the suction, so a friend, Alfie Harcus, stood in front with a piece of smoking rag and they watched the smoke being drawn into the revolving propeller.

Jim got a present of an old mahogany table top and from it fashioned a special propeller. "This is definitely the best one yet," he thought. It was late one night, way past bedtime when he finished it, but Jim could not wait until the next evening, he would have to try it now. In his hurry, he forgot to fit in the split pin to hold the nut in place. The result was a disaster. He revved up the engine, the nut flew off and so did the propeller, which bounced and danced about the end of the workshop. That was the end of the special propeller and Jim thought it was as well Alfie had not been standing in front of it with a smoking rag.

About this time, the Berry folks were building a new byre and barn. Wood was very scarce so they bought a disused gutter's hut in Bressay, intending to use the wood for a roof and doors for their new building. While they were dismantling the hut, Jim noticed that

First plane. Courtesy Jim Smith

the built-in bunks were of really good quality timber. The boards were straight-grained and mostly free from knots. He realised that this wood would make ideal struts for his proposed plane, so it was removed very carefully and laid aside.

With his knowledge of aerodynamics and aeroplanes, Jim had been designing the plane he would build. When the build started he frequently had visitors from the village and elsewhere coming to watch this exciting project proceed. I remember being there among the many spectators and I took several photos. The plane had a wood frame covered with fabric, and the Austin 7 engine, now with another propeller securely fitted in place. It took about three years to build, all done in the evenings when the day's work was over. When it was finished, Jim took the plane out to a park when there were no spectators about, started up the engine, got in, revved up, and said, "Now, let's see what you can do."

The plane motored along the park, made a few jumps, then gave a good high bounce. Unfortunately, a fence got in the way so the project was abandoned.

Undaunted, Jim decided to try again. While reading a popular flying magazine he saw an advert for plans for a French single-seat plane – a D31 Turbulent – fitted with a Volkswagen car engine. He

Under construction. Photo: Clement J. Williamson. Courtesy Jim Smith.

The Flying Farmer

sent for the plans, then for the wood, glue and all the very necessary bits and pieces. Again, it took about three years, with lots of ups and downs, before it was finished. When painted, it was a really lovely looking plane and Jim was very well pleased with the result of his labours. He said all kinds of interesting people came to Berry wanting to see how the plane was progressing. One of these was a BEA Viscount captain called Rocky Stone. He was very interested in gliders and light aircraft and told Jim that before he joined BEA he had been a test pilot with Hawkers. If Jim would permit him, he would like to test fly this plane. Jim thought that was a splendid idea, as at that moment in time he did not have a pilot's licence, so Captain Stone told Jim he would phone when he was going to be at Sumburgh again.

One day some time after this, they were dipping sheep at Berry when Jim's mother came out and said Rocky Stone was on the phone. Captain Stone informed Jim that he would be at Sumburgh the next day and if he could have the little plane at the end of the

Careful now. Photo: Clement J. Williamson. Courtesy Jim Smith.

Willie's Tales & Travels

At airport. Photo: Clement J. Williamson. Courtesy Jim Smith.

Waiting. Photo: Clement J. Williamson. Courtesy Jim Smith.

runway, with the engine running, he would give it a test flight. Jim asked a friend who had a lorry to come to Berry and they got the plane on the lorry and set off for Sumburgh. The plane was unloaded, wheeled into position at the end of a runway, and the engine started, just as Captain Stone landed the Viscount. Friends, photographers and curious onlookers were all hovering around; there was no overdone security at Sumburgh in those days. Captain Stone hurried across from the Viscount, talked briefly to Jim, and walked twice around the little plane. He then climbed into the cockpit, got himself comfortably seated and fastened the seat belt, gave Jim a thumbs up sign, then opened the throttle and, in less time than it takes to tell, the little plane was in the air. The call sign was BW – Bravo Whisky.

Coming in to land. Photo: Clement J. Williamson. Courtesy Jim Smith.

Jim at the controls. Photo: Clement J. Williamson. Courtesy Jim Smith.

It was a wonderful sensation for Jim to see his plane leave the ground, climb into the air and fly over the airfield. As the plane climbed, banked and circled overhead, all thoughts of the many hours spent on the construction were gone. Rocky Stone flew around a few times then landed and told Jim he was very impressed with the plane's performance and had no doubt concerning its airworthiness for certificates. Jim got his pilot's licence and in his spare time spent many happy hours flying around the Sumburgh area.

Whenever he had the plane out he said there was always someone there who had a pilot's licence and wanted to fly it. On one occasion, Jim and Willie Peterson were going to Aberdeen on farming business. In the hut at Sumburgh (there were no huge buildings at Sumburgh Airport then) one of the firemen came and asked Jim if he would come and start his plane.

"Why do you want my plane started?" Jim asked.

The fireman replied that a Viscount captain wanted to have a flight. Jim said that the captain was already seated in his plane, looking very embarrassed as he had not asked permission. "If you let me fly your plane, I will let you have a go at the controls of the Viscount on the way to Aberdeen" he said.

Jim Smith's plane. Photo: Clement J. Williamson. Courtesy Jim Smith.

Jim thought it was a joke, and laughed. He soon got the engine started and the captain flew around the airfield and complimented Jim on the little plane.

Jim and Willie were seated together on the Viscount and after they had been in the air for 20 minutes or so the captain came and asked Jim if he would now like to fly the Viscount. Jim was surprised, as he had thought the captain had been joking, but Willie was alarmed. "You can't let him fly a great big plane like this. He is just used with a small plane," he said, but Jim took the controls of the Viscount for a time, and said that it was like driving a truck compared to the little plane.

Bravo Whisky was sold eventually to a flying club in Aberdeenshire but, unfortunately, is no more, as it met a sad end in a field. It was quite an achievement to build a plane on a farm and to be able to fly it. A very clever and able man is Jim Smith MBE.

THE VANISHING COD

"WE'VE HAD a splendid dinner today, cod done in the oven with roast fat over it. Man it was really good," said my workmate, Jeck, when we arrived back at our work one day after lunch.

"Just where did you get a cod?" I asked.

In Scalloway at that time there was no shop selling fish to the householder. Fish was landed at the pier and sold by auction. It was

The author (left) and Peerie Jeck, early 1950s.

The Vanishing Cod

bought by dealers and, for the most part, shipped south. You could buy fish from Lowrie Williamson's factory at West Shore, where they were filleted and smoked, and some folk did, however, it was more usual for men to visit boats at the pier and get a 'fry', as it was called. Those of us who were not in the habit of getting a fry, including Jeck, did not eat so much fish.

"I'll tell dee where the cod came from," said Jeck, "but du must not tell anyone."

I promised the utmost secrecy and Jeck started to tell all.

"Last night was fine and quiet so I thought I would wander down to Blacksness," he said. "Going along the New Street, I saw Aald Peter ahead of me and as he talks ten to the dozen about anything and nothing in particular, I decided not to get too close to him. When I walked around the corner of Blacksness Shop and along the West Side of the pier, Aald Peter was heading for a fishing boat. The men in the boat were gutting fish and throwing the guts over the side. The seagulls [as was commonplace at that time] were having a great time feeding [the gulls nowadays are starving, as gutting is not allowed in the harbour area] and I stopped to watch them. The boat's engine was running and above the noise I heard one of the men on the boat ask Aald Peter if he would like a fry. 'Oh, thank you, thank you,' replied Peter. 'That would be fine,' and a large cod was thrown up on the pier.

Herring curing, west side, Blacksness. Photo: Clement J. Williamson

Willie's Tales & Travels

"Well, Willie, du kens, Aald Peter was not likely to refuse a cod. That would be two days dinner for him and his wife, and a bit to salt as well. So Aald Peter was most profuse in his thanks and wished them well for the rest of the week. Gathering up the cod, he wandered away in the direction of the steamer's store and, for some reason, I wandered after him. My reason, whatever it was,

Good catch of cod. Photo: Clement J. Williamson

turned out to be a good one for me. Aald Peter walked along the south side of the store and I now thought he was going to go up the road and head for home. But instead, he headed across the road to W.S. Uncle's fish sheds, where a lot of fish boxes were stacked along a wall. Peter looked around him, then eased up a fish box and carefully laid the cod into the box below. When I saw this I hurried back along the steamer's store and stood where Tammie Henry's oil tank was, wondering what Peter was going to do now.

"Well, Willie, I soon found out. He had seen another fishing boat approaching the pier. Aald Peter may have been old, but he hurried to take the boat's rope and get it fixed to a ring. Some of the men greeted him, and he asked the usual questions, but his real interest was the big haddocks lying on the deck. So Peter was not long in asking for a fry. One of the crew told him to come aboard and string some up for himself. This he did, and when I saw that he had six big haddocks on the string, I made off in the direction of W.S. Uncle's fish sheds. After making sure that no one was looking, I lifted up the fish box, took the cod and hurried up the road to the house as fast as I could. That's how I came to have a lovely piece of cod for my dinner. Now don't tell. Does du hear me? Just imagine

Curing herring, east side pier and showing W.S. Uncle's shed. Photo: Clement J. Williamson

it, Willie, him hunting through all the fish boxes. That's what greed does for you boy."

Jeck stopped speaking for a moment, then said, "Willie, there is only one thing that I am really vexed about." Jeck's face was very serious, and I wondered if he was having second thoughts about taking the old man's cod, but then he smiled, "That I was not there to see his face when he lifted up the fish box and the cod had vanished."

PEERIE CHARLIE'S PEATS

THIS IS A YARN I heard many years ago concerning Peerie Charlie, who stayed at the top of Houl. My memories of Charlie are from when he burned coal which he carried, a quarter of a hundredweight at a time, from Nicolson & Co.'s to the top of Houl. However, many years earlier Charlie had worked peats.

Charlie had his peat bank in the North Hill, as did a lot of other Scalloway folk. One day a man in an adjacent bank noticed that some of his peats seemed to be missing while Charlie's seemed to have increased in number. It was reported and investigated and Charlie was charged with stealing peats. He vehemently denied the charge saying, "My, my. Who would ever do such a thing as to steal someone's peats?"

So Charlie duly appeared at the Sheriff court in Lerwick. The charge was read out, but Charlie still maintained his innocence. "Na, na, you ken. As for tae steal somebody's peats. Na, na, I never would do such a thing."

Nevertheless, Charlie was found guilty, and the Sheriff announced that stealing peats was disgraceful conduct and would not be tolerated. He would fine Charlie one pound, or sentence him to thirty days. Charlie replied, "So, so, dan. I'll just take the pound."

It was explained to Charlie that he had to part with the pound or go to prison. But Charlie had no money so some local person came forward and paid the fine. That seemed to be the end of the matter, with everyone knowing that Charlie took the peats and Charlie to the last denying it.

One day, some time later, Charlie was walking along the street when he met Walter Mowat senior, who said, "Charlie, this is a terrible thing that you are being accused of, stealing peats." Charlie agreed and said that indeed it was a terrible accusation to put on an old but honest man. Walter stepped closer, looked from right to left and, lowering his voice, said, "But Charlie, how did they know it was you that took the peats?"

Charlie looked from right to left and, lowering his voice, replied, "You see, they found the marks of my barrow wheel."

Lowrie Halcrow of Blydoit, so the story goes, took pity on Charlie and gave him the use of a rig to grow potatoes. Charlie dug the rig and set seed, and as the tatties grew he would set off from Houl with his hoe to try to keep them weed free. When tatties formed Charlie would sometimes take a few home with him, as small new tatties were very tasty. The rig next to Charlie's was Lowrie's tattie rig, and one day Charlie could not resist looking to see how Lowrie's tatties were progressing. They were forming nicely so Charlie helped himself to some. He thought he was a smart guy and made sure the shows were replaced and that all looked normal. But one day, Lowrie happened to come around and saw Charlie among his tatties. He made all haste towards Charlie and let him hear some choice words – now I never heard Lowrie, but have it on good authority that his swearing vocabulary was not to be equalled. Needless to say, that was the end of Charlie having a rig of tatties on Lowrie's croft.

Lowrie's house. Photo: Clement J. Williamson

HOLIDAY VISIT

WHEN OUR two bairns were at university and college, Vera and I would go down to Scotland twice a year to spend a little time with them. We would also stay for a time in Banchory, beside Vera's mother. On one of those occasions my mother-in-law, Amie, said she had told a friend that we would be arriving shortly and the friend had said she would be awfully pleased if we would call one evening, as she would like to meet us. So one Sunday, Amie announced that we would call on her friend that evening. Being out through the day and having a very late tea, it was after nine o' clock before we set off for the visit.

It was August, and though not dark, the daylight was fading when we reached the friend's house. The street was very quiet and the only light to be seen in the house came from an upstairs window. The curtains were drawn, and I could see that part of the top half of the window was open. I said to mother-in-law that the folk surely had gone to bed so maybe we should leave it until another night. "No, no," she said, "We are here now and we have been invited," and rang the doorbell.

I was standing back looking up at the lighted window when suddenly the curtain was thrown back and a woman looked down at us. Possibly unaware that the window was open, she announced in a loud voice to whoever else was in the room. "Ma Christ, it's thae bloody folk fae Shetland," and closed the curtain.

"That's it," I said. "Let's get out of here."

Mother-in-law, however, was made of much sterner stuff and stood her ground. "We have been invited," she said, and so we waited to see what, if anything, was going to happen.

Then a light appeared in the door and soon the lady of the house appeared clad in a fancy dressing gown. "My, how lovely to see you. Do come in. I have been so looking forward to meeting you."

She took us into the sitting room, switched on the light, and went to the window to pull the curtains. The settee stood just before the window, and onto this she climbed, grabbed a curtain, which was made of a rather heavy material, and pulled. What followed next was like a scene out of one of the silent films of a bygone age. The curtain, complete with curtain rail, suddenly came adrift from its moorings and enveloped the woman as she sagged to her knees. With the strain now on the other half of the curtain rail it too gave way and descended. Trying not to laugh at this hilarious scene, Vera and I rushed to the rescue. We got the dishevelled woman clear of the curtains then set about getting it all put to rights. With Vera taking the weight of the rather heavy material, I got the clips all back in place and we gently closed the curtain.

THE VIEWING

AT ONE TIME in Shetland nearly every district had its own undertaker, who was a joiner or woodworker with a small workshop. A crofter named Lowrie had the workshop in this story, and he was assisted by his neighbour, Jeemsie, also a crofter. Lowrie and Jeemsie were the two most unlikely undertakers you could imagine. Lowrie had a great sense of humour and Jeemsie was a prankster, so there was always laughter when the two were together, except for solemn occasions like the laying out or the kystin (placing the body in a coffin) of a deceased.

On one particular occasion, they were called to a house where an old lady had passed away. While in the house, they were told that her nephew, Dodie, was on a bender in Lerwick and had not been home for nigh on two weeks. This was not news to them as it was common talk in the district. They commiserated and hoped he would come home soon, and left the house saying they would return the next evening with the coffin.

The same day, after two weeks on the booze, Dodie was picked up by the police for his own safety. The two policemen were Shetland men and knew Dodie well, so they took him to the station, wrapped him in blankets and put him to bed in a cell. It was fortunate that the chief constable was on holiday. Next evening, as Dodie appeared to have sobered up a bit and had eaten some food, they decided to put him home.

They arrived at the croft house just as Lowrie and Jeemsie emerged after the kystin. Lowrie told the two policemen that it was good of them to bring Dodie home, and especially at this sad time when his aunt had died. Jeemsie took Dodie's arm and said to him, "How are you feeling, just as frisky as ever, Dodie?"

Dodie peered at Jeemsie through an alcoholic haze and said, "Yes, yes, I'm sure of it."

One of the constables said to Lowrie that it would perhaps be better if he and Jeemsie took Dodie into the house. Lowrie agreed and the policemen then left. Jeemsie, with a glint in his eye, said, "Dodie, we have just been kystin your Aunty Baabie, and we wondered if you would like to view the remains?"

This took a couple of minutes or so to get through his alcohol-fogged brain, then Dodie straightened himself up, squared his shoulders and replied, "Yes, yes, poor Aunty Baabie. Yes, yes."

Jeemsie, instead of heading for the house, steered Dodie towards Dodie's own workshop. This was a large shed used for woodworking, general repairs and storage, and with which Jeemsie and Lowrie were well acquainted. Lowrie wondered what devilment Jeemsie was planning. They went into the workshop and Lowrie switched on the light, while Jeemsie and Dodie headed for a tool chest that stood along a wall. Lowrie could now read Jeemsie's mind so, with great reverence, he slowly lifted the lid of the tool chest. As Dodie peered into a collection of tools, hammers, chisels, planes and screwdrivers, Jeemsie said, "She is very like herself, isn't she Dodie?"

Dodie lifted his head, looked at Jeemsie, then back at the tool chest. Lowrie, his voice verging on hysteria, said, "She is so peaceful looking, you would almost think she was sleeping."

At that, Dodie put his hands over his face and cried out, "Oh my God, my poor Aunty Baabie."

Lowrie hurriedly lowered the lid of the chest and they left the shed. On reaching the house, they quietly opened the door and pushed Dodie in. Closing the door gently, they quickly got into Lowrie's van and, with howls of laughter, sped away as fast as the side road would permit.

Local knowledge had it that Dodie never touched alcohol for at least six month after the viewing.

REGATTA TIMES

Scalloway regatta, late 1940s - early 1950s. Photo: Clement J. Williamson

REGATTAS were both competitive events and social outings. Folks who had probably never seen each other since the last regatta would meet for a long exchange of news, while others were mainly interested in the sailing. In the pre-sixties and pre-war days the boats were all Shetland models. There were no Maids, Fireballs, or other fast little boats that skim across the water. Boats came from Whiteness, Weisdale, Skeld, Reawick, Burra Isle, Walls, Sand, Lerwick and, of course, Scalloway. One photo shows 19 Shetland model boats lined up at Blacksness pier; a sight never to be seen again.

It was a time of great excitement and expectation at Blacksness Pier when the boats were getting ready. The noise of sails flapping, men shouting and people rushing to get a better view, time keepers checking watches, handicaps being set, and everyone hurrying

Willie's Tales & Travels

Shetland model boats, 1930s. Photo: Clement J. Williamson

about. Shore skippers gave their considered opinions as to the outcome, and there were small boys wishing they too could be a member of a crew. It was very exciting, even to a landlubber.

On regatta day, many houses in Scalloway had lots of visitors at lunch time. There were no cafes in the village, so folk visited friends. Our folk at West Shore always made a large pot of soup so friends and relations from Burra and Whiteness could have soup, sandwiches, and a cup of tea. There was a lot of talk, as stories were told about what had happened over the past year, and lots of laughter, of course. It was a jolly time and fine to look back on and remember.

I remember Blacksness Pier thronged with people, some watching the sailing and others watching the swimming events. There would be men with binoculars hanging round their necks and some with a spy-glass in a jacket pocket; others had a half bottle in their jacket pocket or in a hip pocket.

One unfortunate spectator with a half bottle in his hip pocket took a step back and fell. Young boys are quick to notice anything out of the ordinary, and when they saw two men helping the unfortunate spectator towards a pile of fish boxes, they followed. The man was laid across some boxes, his trousers and pants taken down and his bare backside exposed. As far as we could see there were no serious cuts, just scratches; he was lucky.

"Just tell me it's blood, boys," he said, in hope. With much laughter from the two men, slivers of glass were removed from his skin and pieces of the bottle from his pants. Soon he was on his feet, unsteady but none the worse.

REGATTA TIMES

Girl on greasy pole. Photo: Clement J. Williamson

Start of tub race, 1930s. Photo: Clement J. Williamson

Willie's Tales & Travels

Pillow fight at pier. Bertie Burgess puts them down. Photo: Clement J. Williamson

Ladies' race, 1930s. Photo: Clement J. Williamson

REGATTA TIMES

Scalloway regatta, 1950s. Photo: Clement J. Williamson

The sailing enthusiasts never left the pier area all day long except for a quick bite of lunch. Many discussions were held as to what some skipper or other should have done; if only he had done this or that he would have won. Indeed, many a race would be recalled over and over again in the ensuing weeks.

WILLIE'S TALES & TRAVELS

The swimming events, which were held on the north side of the pier, were always good entertainment. The pillow fights, greasy pole, tub races, and swimming and diving drew great crowds. There was a lot of fun and laughter as some of the swimmers would play-act to the crowd, and people cheered for their favourite swimmers. Sadly, those aquatic events are no longer to be seen at regattas.

I heard the following yarn many years ago. It was a fine pre-war regatta day, with sunshine for the shore folk and a good breeze for the sailing men. A lot of boats were competing in the afternoon and there was intense excitement among the pier-head skippers. Among the crowd, and just as interested in the sailing, was the local police constable of the day (if I heard his name mentioned, and I probably did, I don't remember it). When the boats left the pier and were heading out of the harbour he, like a lot of others, took a seat on some fish boxes in the lea of the steamer's store. As it was a fine warm day he undid the buttons on his tunic. He got out his pipe and filled it with tobacco, set a match to it and leaned back, tilting his peaked cap forward to keep the sun out of his eyes. It was a perfect day, but alas would not be so for long.

Hit the post, 1930s. Photo: Clement J. Williamson

48

Regatta Times

    Meanwhile, over at the park the land sports were in full swing. The sun was shining, there was a large crowd, bairns were laughing and the races were under way. Everything was just as it should be except for two men who were the worse of drink and were making a proper nuisance of themselves. They were getting in the way of bairns racing, and trying to join in the races. When an official tried to remonstrate with them and get them off the field, one of them became abusive and challenged everyone to fight. What had been funny was now a nasty situation.

    Then a car came down the New Road and parked on the Burn Beach. A well-dressed man and his wife got out of the car and made their way up the New Road. The man was the sheriff from Lerwick. A lot of people were standing at the dyke overlooking the park and the sheriff and his wife joined them. At that same moment, a regatta official was trying to get the drunks out of the way so a bairns' race could start. The two drunks were waving their arms and shouting abuse. The sheriff turned to one of the spectators and said, "I thought you had a police constable in Scalloway?"

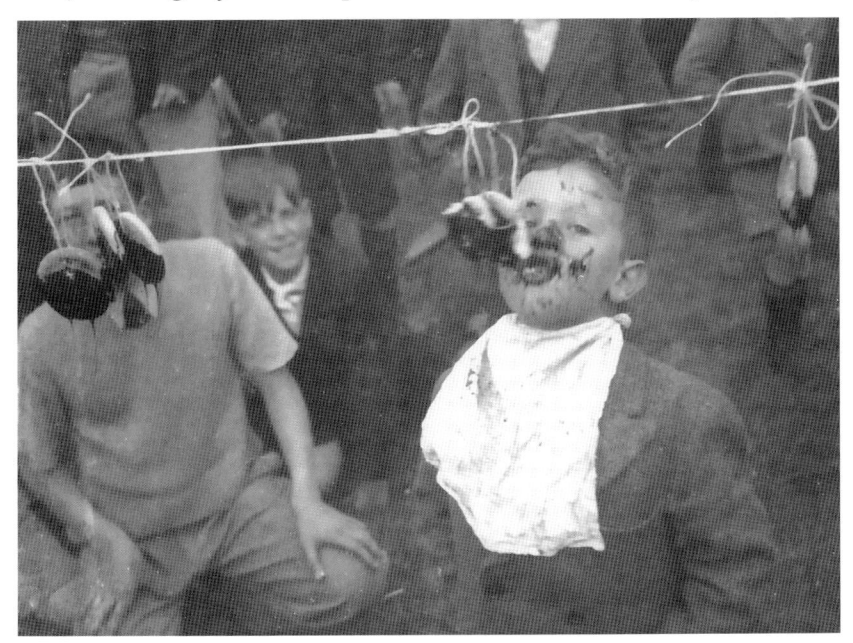

Treacle biscuit, 1930s. Photo: Clement J. Williamson

Willie's Tales & Travels

"Oh, we do," was the reply, "but he is down at Blacksness Pier watching the sailing."

The sheriff spoke briefly to his wife then set off for the pier. Rounding a corner of the steamer's store, he observed all the pierhead skippers and among them, seated like the others on a fish box, was the police constable. With the warmth from the sun and the hubbub of voices around him the constable was feeling comfortable, contented and drowsy. Suddenly his sleepy eyes became aware of a pair of highly polished brown shoes and, squinting up against the sun, he saw with dismay the sheriff standing in front of him.

"So this is where you are, sitting here in the sun. Good God, man, don't you know that up in the park bottoms are being kicked?" said the sheriff.

The constable hurriedly sprang to his feet, put away his pipe, straightened his hat and fastened his tunic. Mumbling, "Yes sir, yes sir," he headed up Blacksness Brae at a half run.

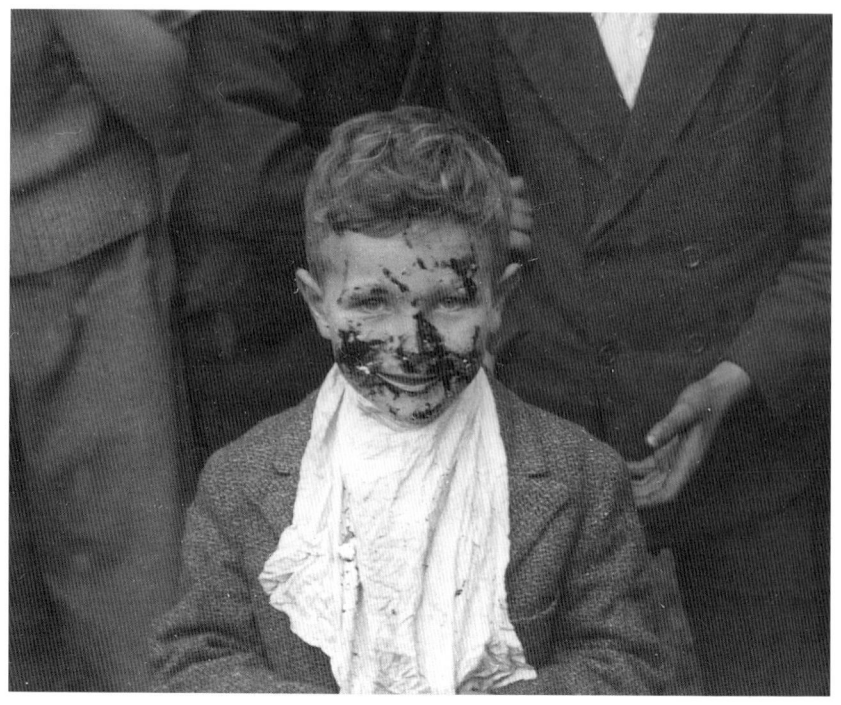

Oh Jim! 1930s. Photo: Clement J. Williamson

REGATTA TIMES

Lerwick lass, 1950s. Photo: Willie Smith

When, a bit out of breath, he reached the park nothing seemed to be out of place. All was peaceful, with bairns racing, people sitting in the sun, and no sign of any bottoms being kicked. Wondering if it had all been a bad dream, he made enquiries. It transpired that one of the regatta officials had delivered an ultimatum to the worst of the two offenders: behave or accept the consequences. The belligerent drunk chose not to behave so the official delivered the consequences – two hard jabs where it hurt most. Both drunks then left the park immediately. The police constable, huffing and puffing

Willie's Tales & Travels

Pillow fight at Fraser Park 1950s. Bertie Burgess puts them down. Photo: Clement J. Williamson

Cruise with M/B Tirrick 1950s. Photo: Clement J. Williamson

Regatta Times

Girls' race. Photo: Clement J. Williamson

Sack race. Photo: Clement J. Williamson

WILLIE'S TALES & TRAVELS

Tossing the caber. Photo: Clement J. Williamson

Three-legged race, 1950s. Photo: Clement J. Williamson

after his hurried trip from Blacksness, said what he intended to do about the two drunks, but the official insisted it was all over and best forgotten. And so it was, at the time, but the yarn is still remembered after all those years.

Regatta 1950s. Photo: Clement J. Williamson

THE DEEP DIVE

I NEVER SAW the deep dive as it had been banned years before my time, but I heard stories about it from my brother-in-law, Clement Williamson.

At the regatta swimming events, a raft was placed at the pier for the swimmers and officials (the raft belonged to Hay & Co., Blacksness, for use by carpenters working at boats). The year was 1922 and on the raft this particular regatta day were Harry Williamson, Laurence Mowat and Clement Williamson. Several swimmers entered for the deep dive, which was a contest to see who could remain underwater for the longest period of time. It was exciting for the spectators. From the pier they could – if the water was calm enough – make out the form of the swimmers moving about under water. They all got applause when they surfaced and their times were noted by the timekeeper on the raft.

The last to enter this day was a Scalloway man, Willie Sinclair, a seaman. He took his place on the raft, dived in and disappeared below the surface. When he hit the water the stopwatch was on. The seconds ticked by and no one was concerned until 40 seconds or so had passed. Then a minute went by, and someone shouted that he must have come up under the raft. Some swimmers jumped in and looked under the raft but he was not there. On the raft, Clement and the others were now concerned, but the stopwatch was still ticking away. On the pier, the spectators were hushed and silent; most were thinking that Willie Sinclair had drowned. Then, after one minute and 45 seconds, the dark hair of Willie broke the surface and he swam slowly to the raft. Clement said a great cheer came from the crowd and they applauded what must have been a record-breaking dive. Clement said he later asked Willie Sinclair how he was able to stay under water so long. He said he did not go swimming about, using up his air like the others had been doing, but swam to the bottom and took hold of anything he could find to anchor him down. There he sat, conserving his breath until he

The Deep Dive

had just enough air to take him to the surface. This worked well for Willie at Scalloway, but nearly cost him his life a few weeks later at the Lerwick regatta swimming sports.

When the deep dive was called, Willie was there, and when it came to his turn, he dived as usual and disappeared below the surface. When about a minute had ticked away the crowd on the pier, knowing of his record dive at Scalloway, were not unduly worried. Then the top of Willie's head broke the surface for a second, and sank again. He was in trouble and all on the pier knew it. Several Lerwick swimmers dived down as far as they could but did not locate him. Among the crowd on the pier that day was Charles Stout, a Lerwick chemist. He was a very fine underwater swimmer and without hesitation dived at the spot where Willie Sinclair had last been seen. The crowd watched anxiously as the seconds ticked by, and then Charles Stout appeared with Willie in his arms. He had been to the bottom for him. Other swimmers jumped in to help and soon Willie was on the pier, deeply unconscious.

Very fortunately for Willie, that day among the crowd was the Lerwick Baptist minister, Rev. Fotheringham, who held a medical degree. He now came forward and applied artificial respiration. To the delight and relief of the large crowd Willie coughed and opened his eyes; he was alive. But for the fortunate presence on the pier that day of Charles Stout and Rev. Fotheringham the deep dive could have had a very disastrous ending.

Clement said he later asked Willie what had happened that day and Willie said the water at the Lerwick pier was much deeper than at Scalloway. That day, on the way to the surface, his air had run out and he had breathed in water.

After this near tragedy the deep dive was very wisely dropped from future swimming events.

CHIEF ABADOU

IN THE SUMMER OF, I believe 1937, a travelling fair came to Lerwick and set up camp at Grantfield. It was a great attraction, with many tents and stalls, and stallholders shouting to come and try their entertainments. Another time there was a Wall of Death show. I never actually saw it but was told it was a round wooden drum-like structure about 15 or 20 feet high. I don't know how wide it was. They ran motor bikes inside this, and the show consisted of the motor bike riders mounting the sloping area at the bottom and then, with speed building up, going round and round right up the perpendicular wall to the top, and then back down to the bottom and safety. The paying audience stood at the top looking in over (there must have been a safety rail). As far as I remember, it was in Lerwick for just one year. After that, there was a story about a rider on the mainland being killed when a door opened.

At Scalloway regatta time, some of the entertainers relocated their tents and stalls to the village park for an afternoon. I remember one stall had air rifles, and if you hit two bulls out of three you won a prize. However, the rifles were so poor that you should have been given a prize for hitting the target, never mind the bull. Another stall had three white enamel pails set at an angle. For threepence you got three table tennis balls and you had to try and get them all in the pails for a prize. All the people I saw try this threw the balls in the pails (it looked so easy), but they promptly bounced straight out again. The secret was to get the balls to hit inside the rim of the pail, so that they ran round inside and stayed there. It was easy money for the stallholder!

The show I remember most was a black African called Chief Abadou. I had never seen a dark-skinned man before and wanted to get a closer look. He stood outside his tent on some boxes with a barker, who shouted, "Roll up, roll up, see the African chieftain who can eat fire and dance on broken glass. Chief Abadou will amaze and thrill you with his African magic."

CHIEF ABADOU

I decided I would have to see this act. It was going to cost a sixpence, a lot of money for an eight-year-old boy to have. By the time I had persuaded one of my sisters to give me a sixpenny piece,

Chief Abadou. Photo: Clement J. Williamson

people were crowded into the tent for the show. (I was very small as a child and only really started to grow when I was 12 or 13. I was consequently known as Peerie Willie, and even as a five-foot-eleven teenager a local man still always addressed me as Peerie Willie, as if it was a double-barrelled name.)

I paid my sixpence and went into the tent. A lot of people had gone in before me and as there was no way I was going to see anything, I started to push my way in among the legs until I was right at the front. After a short wait, the barker and Chief Abadou appeared and climbed onto a small stage, most probably built from wooden fish boxes; very versatile things fish boxes. The barker recited a long spiel about Chief Abadou and where he came from and what he could do. I don't remember much about that part. Then came his first feat of magic – fire eating. A flaming brand was waved about for all to see before disappearing into the chief's mouth. When it reappeared it was still burning. He did this a time or two, and it looked very impressive.

Chief Abadou. Photo: Clement J. Williamson

The barker then said that the chief was going to dance on broken glass and that this would amaze us. The glass was in a box right by where I was standing and it certainly looked like broken glass. The barker asked if someone would like to examine the glass box. Davie Umphray was standing alongside me so he looked, then announced that it was indeed broken glass. The barker spoke again about the magic and that Chief Abadou's feet would be uninjured in any way. He asked if someone would like to examine the chief's feet. Again it was Davie Umphray, who by this time was kneeling alongside the box of glass. Chief Abadou held out his left foot and Davie took hold of his ankle. There was nothing on the chief's foot and Davie tickled his instep with a finger. The chief gave the same reaction as anyone else would have done and yanked his foot away. Davie laughed and said, "Boys, I can assure you there is nothing on his feet."

The barker had some more to say, then Chief Abadou stepped into the box of broken glass and started to dance and chant. The glass crunched and crumpled and sounded like it was breaking up. With the wild yells of the chief it was all too much for me and I started to feel sick. I had to push my way between the tightly packed legs to get outside, where I almost threw up. Was it worth a sixpence? I don't know.

Here I digress a little with a modern foot and glass story. One day in the 1970s, I was walking along Main Street, in front of the Church of Scotland. Looking seaward I saw a young boy sitting among the seaweed on the beach. This was an odd place to be sitting, I thought. The boy had taken off a slipper and was now pulling off his sock, so I stopped to see what he was going to do next. When his sock came off I saw blood on his foot, so I shouted, "What's happened to you?"

"I've cut my foot on a broken bottle," he answered. I went down the steps beside the old water pump and had a look at his foot. It had a cut on the sole but didn't look too serious. Handing him his slipper and sock, I picked him up and carried him up to the road. I set him on the dyke, went back along the street for my van, and put him home. That boy is now taller, thicker, broader, heavier and stronger than me. I certainly would not like to try and carry Ronnie (Biscuit) Leask very far today.

On the night of the Scalloway Fire Festival, 2011, Willie tries, unsuccessfully, to lift Ronnie Biscuit and his torch. Photo: William C.T. Smith

REGATTA MUSIC

Lerwick Pipe Band, 1939. Photo: Clement J. Williamson

EVERYONE WHO liked good music looked forward to regatta day. Musicians would come from various country districts with fiddles, accordions and guitars. Even from Scotland, bands would come to busk and earn a few pounds. Previous to my recollection there were bands such as Caldwell's Band and Morayshire Melody Makers. I can just recall Curly McKay's Band, but the musicians I remember best were George Stark playing fiddle and Willie Jordan playing guitar. George had been blind since a young lad and was known affectionately in Shetland as 'da blind fiddler'. He was a visitor to Shetland for over 50 years. Wherever he played a crowd would always gather round to listen, and you could see his white bow flickering above their heads. He introduced lots of new tunes to the Shetlanders, and they in turn soon learned to play them.

I remember at one regatta sports event in the Fraser Park, a lot of us boys were sitting around on the grass listening to George playing his fiddle and Willie with his guitar. When they finished a selection I said, "Play wis da *Banks*, Geordie."

WILLIE'S TALES & TRAVELS

Curly McKay Band. Photo: Clement J. Williamson

Band on New Street. Photo: Clement J. Williamson

Regatta Music

George Stark and Willie Jordan, 1950s. Photo: Clement J. Williamson

He turned his sightless eyes in my direction and replied, "You're asking me to work hard for my money, laddie." Needless to say, he played the *Banks* and the *High Level*, both hornpipes, and got money in the hat.

George Stark and Auld Dey o Havra play at Scalloway regatta, 1930s. Photo: Clement J. Williamson

WILLIE'S TALES & TRAVELS

One year he had a grandson with him who played the accordion. My brother-in-law, Clement Williamson, got the three of them in The Studio and made a recording on the first tape recorder in Scalloway, a Baird. I still have that original recording, done on a reel-to-reel tape at seven and a half inches per second.

Da blind fiddler entertains. Photo: Clement J. Williamson

Regatta Music

Another fine regatta day, among the folks from Burra Isle was Joe Laurenson. Joe, an accomplished musician, had his accordion with him and, as he was walking by The Studio, Clement suggested he stop and play a few tunes. Joe sat on The Studio dyke and played and in less time than it takes to tell, a small crowd had gathered. Then, down from the Braehead came another accomplished accordion player, Walter Mowat Jnr. Walter had his accordion with him and took a seat beside Joe on the dyke. Sailing, swimming and sports were forgotten by the crowd gathered at The Studio. Many were the requests for tunes and many were played.

I recall Joe playing a tune that day which he called *Pedro's Return*, a tune that involved a lot of bass hand work. I have never heard anyone else play it, but would certainly like to hear it again. The music was superb and much appreciated. What a pity there were no video cameras in those days.

Joe Laurenson and Walter Mowat. Photo: Clement J. Williamson

Wis dan, 1950s: Alistair Thomson, Jim Halcrow, the author.

Wis noo, 2009. Alistair, Jim, the author. Photo: William C.T. Smith

Regatta Music

Regatta concerts were always a great attraction and outside the hall there would be a queue before the doors were opened. Various local musicians would take part and do their best and always got good applause. One time, some local lasses had learned Highland dances and danced the Sword Dance and the Highland Fling.

On another occasion, some local lads, myself included, were to play and it was suggested that a smoker from the National Kippering Kiln might perform with us. He was a good singer and might sing some 'cowboy songs', as they were then called. He agreed and turned up at the rehearsal and sang three songs, and it went well. On regatta night, however, he arrived at the hall obviously the worse of drink. The lady organising the concert was not at all pleased, and a discussion took place as to whether to let him onto the stage or not. He was quite sure of himself and said, "Nae bother, nae bother," and insisted on performing. With the obvious help from 'Johnnie Walker', he was a great success, and not a microphone or loudspeaker to be seen. The crowd loved his singing (and our playing I hope), but when the three songs were finished his ego was now so inflated he was not going to stop; and worse, the crowd wanted more. He then announced what he would sing next, but none of us had heard the song. After that came another unknown song so we all walked off stage except Jim Halcrow, as the smoker was by his side and had started to sing. Jim, the good musician, accompanied him through with the song then, amidst applause, someone closed the curtain.

At another regatta I remember meeting some friends and asking if they were going to the concert that night. "Na," was the reply. "It's just the same old faces every time, and you know what they are going to play and sing."

"Oh well," I remarked, "you will miss Curly. He will be performing tonight."

Now that changed my friend's minds. If Curly was going to be there then so would they. John Jamieson from Sandness, known throughout Shetland as Curly, was a good entertainer. He played the fiddle, but I suppose the best part of his act was his singing accompanied by the guitar and mouth organ. The mouth organ was strapped to the guitar, and Curly would play both instruments at the same time. His act was always very popular.

Willie's Tales & Travels

My son William told me about a concert the 'Shetland Fiddlers' gave in Derby, England. Curly, now a very much older man, did his act with the guitar and mouth organ. William said no one in the audience knew a word Curly said, but he got a tremendous reception. He played a tune which he had composed, telling the audience he had "med him mesel". The result was, as with the National Kiln smoker, Curly did not want to come off the stage. Finally it was done for him when someone closed the curtain.

Curly was a composer of music and among the many tunes he wrote was one for William, called *Smith, the Gallant Fiddler*.

No recollection of music at regattas would be complete without mention of the first disc jockey in Shetland. Bob Smith (or Dobbel as he was usually known), for a few years, played records at the pier in the morning and in the park in the afternoon. The music could be heard all over the village. He had two 12-inch loudspeakers set in four-by-four-foot baffle boards. He had an amplifier and turntable on which he played the 78rpm recordings of the day. The sound quality was excellent, not like the music played through PA systems much later. You could see serious faced men watching the sailing

John Jamieson (Curly).
Photo: William C.T. Smith

Bob Smith.
Photo: Clement J. Williamson

and tapping their feet to music by Jimmy Shand, Jo Stafford or Guy Mitchell. Bob also played his records at dances in the hall where we danced to the same popular hits of the day as did the folks in London. In addition to being a disc jockey, Bob was also an excellent drummer and played with various local bands.

Another accordion player who occasionally entertained at regattas was Bobby Christie, a real local character. Bobby's accordion was the same style as some of the famous Scottish dance band players. In Shetland it was known as a 'Sookie Blaa', or as Bobby called it, 'Da Box'.

Bobby wth box. Courtesy Bobby Christie

DA STUART TURNER

SHETLAND MODEL BOATS fitted with one-and-a-half horsepower engines were used by the Norwegian resistance group based in Scalloway during the Second World War. After the war, these boats were sold to and used by local men, and the one-and-a-half Stuart Turner engines suddenly became very popular. As far as I can remember, the engineering firm of H. Williamson & Son in Scalloway became agents for Stuart Turner engines, and I believe a licence was needed to procure one. Sails were forgotten about as you did not need to rely on the wind to get a Stuart Turner moving, although sometimes you needed some physical wind to get it started.

The engines were fitted in boats all over Shetland and soon people were motoring and putt-putting to places where it was too far to row. Then a four horsepower version became available and was fitted to some of the slightly larger boats. Their superiority over the one-and-a-half engine was that they had a reverse gear. Some one-and-a-half engines also had reverse gear but not many local boats used them, as they were slower.

In the Scalloway area, boats fitted with Stuart Turner engines became so numerous that the local yacht club, which organised the annual regatta, suggested races. So, races were started both for boats with the one-and-a-half, and boats with four horsepower engines.

The one-and-a-half engines were very temperamental, sometimes refusing to start, while at other times they would start with a half turn of the starting handle. One day my neighbour, Cecil Duncan, took us fishing in his boat which was fitted with a one-and-a-half Stuart Turner marine engine, type R3MC, engine number 32967, approximate year 1942/43. We were halfway between two isles when the sound of the engine suddenly went from a purr to a putt-putt, then to a little tinkle, before finally stopping. "What now?" I asked.

Cecil, who was an engineer, said, "Oh, just leave it for five minutes and she will go again no bother." He was right.

Da Stuart Turner

*Cecil with **Kittiwake**'s 1.5hp Stuart Turner. Photo: Willie Smith*

One elderly Shetlander was heard to remark, "The Stuart Turner will get you there but the Hell will it get you back."

Another said, "That one-and-a-half Stuart Turner has put years on me, trying to get the bloody thing started."

They were very temperamental engines.

The race for boats with 1.5hp Stuart Turners. Photo: Clement J. Williamson

73

Willie's Tales & Travels

Cecil fishing aboard Kittiwake. *Courtesy Willis Duncan.*

Da Stuart Turner

The boat *Olav* was, I believe, the first boat in Shetland fitted (by the Shetland Bus men) with a one-and-a-half Stuart Turner. I can remember the men fitting the beds for the engine in the carpenter's shop, then, after the engine was installed, I was taken for a trip around the harbour. It was my first time in a little motorboat, and what a speed it seemed to be going at.

Willie Fullerton bought *Olav* from the Norwegians at the war's end. I remember many years ago, on a fine sunny Sunday afternoon, Willie took a group of people, myself included, to visit one of the isles. I sat amidships and when I put my hand on the gunwale my fingers were in the water. There were no lifebelts, and no one could swim!

The *Olav* is now in the Scalloway Museum.

In the 1950s, there was work to be done at the Bridge End school in Burra Isle, and it had to be done on a Saturday. There was no bridge in those days and I asked Jim Thomson if he would take his boat – a Shetland model fitted with a one-and-a-half Stuart Turner – so that we could work late and hopefully get the job finished. It was a fine morning when we set out but a northerly wind soon set in and by mid-afternoon it was blowing quite strong, so we thought we had

Willie Fullerton aboard Olav. *Photo: Clement J. Williamson*

Willie's Tales & Travels

Bridge End School. Photo: Clement J. Williamson

Jim Thomson. Photo: Willie Smith

Da Stuart Turner

better head back for Scalloway before it got any worse. Between the East and West Isles of Burra it was rough going against the wind, so we decided we would go through Stream Sound and hopefully get some lee from Trondra. Turning north, we realised there was no shelter and there came a squall so powerful that the engine could make no headway. We just stood still for about three or four minutes until the wind eased and we got underway for Scalloway.

Jim Smith, a local farmer, had a larger boat, which had been a ship's lifeboat and later a flit boat in Unst. This he used to transport cattle and sheep to and from the isle of Uyea, which lies off Uyeasound, Unst. The engine in the boat was an eight horsepower Stuart Turner with reverse gear. On one occasion, he had to transport five young cattle to the isle. The boat, which had been lying ashore for some time, developed a bad leak when launched and, as it could not be repaired immediately, he fetched a motor pump, which could contain the leak. "That was fine," said

The Berry boat. Photo: Willie Smith

Willie's Tales & Travels

Jim, "but when you stopped the pump the boat filled with water, so the only thing to do was to keep the pump running."

As the lorry with the cattle was only arriving next morning, Jim decided to stay up all night and see the pump was fuelled and kept running. Next morning all was well; the boat and Jim had spent an uneventful night alongside the West Side pier at Uyeasound. Jim

George Jamieson's boat had an 8hp Stuart with reverse gear. Photo: Willie Smith

and Bobby Fraser, who had arrived from Scalloway to help, put two bales of hay in the bottom of the boat for the cattle to jump on, then waited for the truck to arrive. Soon the cattle were aboard, and they got the Stuart Turner fired up and set off, with the motor pump swishing the incoming water over the side. However, the animals trampled on the hay bales, and soon the water was full of bits of hay, which blocked the pump. With the cattle being forward in the boat, the bow got lower and lower and soon the propeller was out of the water. As they were now not too far from the isle, Jim and Bobby pushed the animals over the side to swim ashore. This lowered the propeller back in the water and somehow the boat, Jim and Bobby, and five young cattle, all reached the isle safely.

It was exciting times owning a Stuart Turner engine.

THE LINO AFFAIR

DURING THE WAR, the Scalloway Public Hall was a military hospital staffed by the Royal Army Medical Corps. Huts were built outside around the hall for wards, and a kitchen and dining rooms inside. At the west side of the hall there was an X-ray unit. This was the second such unit to be based in Scalloway as a doctor who stayed in Dinapore at one time had a unit many years before. The small hall was the operating theatre, and everything was painted with white gloss paint. The lovely pitch pine wall cladding was also white glossed. It was all spotlessly clean and many operations were carried out. For a time the hospital matron was one of the old guard and she ran the place with a very firm hand. All the staff stood in awe of her and were afraid to cross her as she was a formidable lady indeed.

One day, Uncle Robbie and John George Nicolson (who told me this story) were sent to the hospital to lay a piece of lino in a small washroom. Uncle Robbie took along his tool bag with various tools, as one never knew what might be required. They were directed to the washroom and the lino. (I can remember working with the same kind of lino after the war; it was dreadful to work with as it was quarter inch thick and could not bend easily.) The sink in the washroom was of the heavy clay type, measured approximately 36 inches by 22 inches, and stood on a stand with four legs made out of three-by-four-inch wood. The washroom itself, John told me, was not very big and as the door opened into the room they took it off

Scalloway Hall and some huts. Photo: Clement J. Williamson

The Lino Affair

Uncle Robbie.
Photo: Clement J. Williamson

John George Nicolson.

to make movement easier. Uncle Robbie announced that it was not going to be an easy job, and John said he agreed.

They first measured the floor and marked the lino, which was lying in another room. Then there was the problem of fitting the lino around the sink legs. How would they go about this? They got some stiff brown paper and proceeded to make a template. They carried it to the lino and marked around it with a pencil. John said it was not easy to see because the lino was dark brown. Then, with great care, they cut it to size and cut out where the legs would be and everything seemed to be going well. Next, the lino was carefully carried to the washroom and now cuts had to be made so it could be pushed under the sink to see if their cut-outs for the legs were a good fit. It was a ticklish job but it was soon in place. However, a good bit of trimming remained to be done, so Uncle Robbie said they would go and have their lunch and come back at two o'clock to finish it off. They left feeling that they had done a good morning's work.

John said that when he came back to the hut at two o'clock, Uncle Robbie was coming out the door with his tool bag on his back. Thinking that maybe they were going to some other job, he asked what was on. Uncle Robbie just about exploded. "Does du know what dat bloody bitch (Uncle never used words like that as a rule) has done? Come and I'll show dee."

So they went in, and lying partly along a wall in the passage was the piece of lino. About a quarter across one corner was broken, and the area round the carefully cut parts for the sink legs was also broken. The washroom floor was all wet. "She," Uncle Robbie said, "says the floor was supposed to be washed first with disinfectant. Well, why could the stupid woman not have told us that in the morning? I've had enough. Come on back to the workshop."

At the workshop, Uncle Robbie, still fuming, explained to the boss what had happened and said that any so and so could go and finish the job any way they liked. So Uncle Robbie and John were sent to do some other job for the afternoon. Next morning, Uncle Robbie agreed to have another try. "But if that woman," he said, "comes anywhere near us with any nonsense she will get more than she bargains for."

Hospital patients.

The Lino Affair

He and John had to get a new piece of lino, but they had the first piece as a template and fortunately got the job completed without any intervention from matron.

ASSASSINATION ATTEMPT

IN LATE 1939 and the early 1940s, most of the houses in Meadowfield Road were occupied by various army regiments. One house in particular was, for a time anyway, reserved for sergeants only. One day we heard that a soldier had tried to shoot a sergeant. Upon hearing this news, some of us boys hurried immediately to the scene. However, it was all over by the time we arrived and all that we saw was a broken windowpane. A passing soldier, when asked what had happened, was quite willing to tell us.

One of the sergeants, it appeared, was a proper bastard and picked on men for the most trivial of details. An elderly Scalloway woman was walking down Meadowfield Road one day when the sergeant was in full voice. She stopped and listened, then approached the sergeant and gave him a piece of her mind much, I am sure, to the enjoyment of the soldiers.

One soldier was given a particularly hard time, making the poor man's life a proper misery. This soldier was walking up Meadowfield

Meadowfield Road. Photo: Clement J. Williamson

Assassination Attempt

Road that morning and, passing the sergeant's house, he chanced to look at the window. There, standing just inside the window, was the hated sergeant. After enduring weeks of misery and verbal abuse, the soldier lost control of himself and unslung the 303 rifle he carried on his shoulder. He drew back the bolt and a cartridge slipped into the breach. Taking what was obviously a rough aim he fired and broke a windowpane, missing the sergeant who then dived out of sight. While the soldier was trying to reload, some other soldiers who were nearby jumped on him and took his rifle away. What happened to both the soldier and the sergeant we never knew. It was a talking point for quite a long time afterwards, and we did wonder if the sergeant moderated his attitude toward the men he was supposed to be training.

Now, 65 years on, I can still point out the house and the window where the incident took place.

ROBBIE DA DIVER

I STILL REMEMBER many of the folk who stayed in the houses at the top of Westerhoul, including Peerie Charlie and the Hall family. Exactly when Robert (Robbie) Robertson and his wife Christina (Chrissie) moved there, I cannot remember. My older sister Chrissie was friendly with Robbie's wife, who was also called Chrissie, and much visiting took place. I got into the habit of visiting on my own, as I liked Robbie's wife; she played the autoharp and the sound of it fascinated me. She died in February 1945, aged 63 years.

I also visited Robbie in his workshop, which was the house the Hall family had stayed in. He would tell me yarns and give me little jobs to do. I suppose some of the yarns were tall tales, but they were interesting and enthralling to a young boy, and also very believable. He told of diving jobs and looking for wrecks, and of the fish and sharks he had seen. I can remember him diving at Blacksness Pier, but don't recall what he was doing.

One year during the war, there was a heavy fall of snow and Houl Road (da Back Road) was transformed into a splendid place for sledging. On a good run you could go as far as the Tin Sheds or Harcus pier, and with very few cars at that time it was quite safe. There were no gritters to turn the roads to slush, but with all the sledging the road became very smooth and shiny. Willie Laurenson would put a little 'Scord Dust' at the side of the road for folk to walk on but always heeded the bairns' plea of, "Please Willie, not across the road."

One afternoon there were about 20 bairns there with sleds, all having a great time. A few bairns, including myself, had no sled, and had to wait until someone gave them a run. At the top of the brae, Robbie appeared on his way home and he stopped to watch the fun. There was a great rush of sleds going downhill and as Robbie turned to go up to Kiloora he saw me and said, "Willie, do you not have a sledge?" When I said no, his reply was, "Well my boy, you soon will have one."

Next day after school I wondered about what he had said and if he meant it, so I set off for Kiloora. I heard knocking coming from his workshop and wandered in. Sure enough, there on the bench was an almost finished sled, and a beauty it was. The sides were white wood and the top was half round at the front and made of V-lining, which once had graced the walls of a house somewhere. "It will look good when I get it painted," said Robbie.

"No, no," I said. "Never mind painting, I will get it to Lowrie Mowat for steel runners," and so it was. I had many happy hours over the years sledging on that sled, and my bairns and others used it as well. The sled is, as far as I remember, still hanging on the shed wall.

Sometime after Chrissie died, I asked Robbie if he still had the autoharp, which I was willing to purchase. Yes, he told me, it was still in the house and I could have it. I could come along any time. So, one day I went to Kiloora and after tea and biscuits and many yarns he went to get the harp. But what a disappointment it was when the box was opened, the autoharp had got damp and the joints had all opened up. It was completely ruined and would never tune up or play again.

Robbie da diver.

THE GUTTING MACHINE

BOBBY FRASER, a Scalloway fisherman, would sometimes at a weekend visit Berry Farm for a yarn with Jim Smith. Bobby had watched Jim's airplane being built, and had also seen the 'neep lifter' being built and put to work. The neep lifter was towed behind a tractor and, topped, lifted, tailed and deposited the turnips into a trailer. With all this in mind, Bobby said to Jim, "You have made an airplane and made a fine machine for lifting neeps; you are clever, so what's to stop you making a machine to gut fish? It would fairly help us on the boats."

Jim agreed that it would indeed be a very good thing to have on a fishing boat, and so he would think about it. Jim mulled the idea over in his mind, and eventually decided that yes, it could be done.

Fish come in lots of different sizes, so the first step was to find a way to centralise the fish so that the knife or blade would always be in the right position, at the middle of the fish. Then the fish would

Bobby Fraser. Photo: William C.T. Smith

THE GUTTING MACHINE

Jim Smith in plane. Photo: Clement J. Williamson

Jim with neep lifter. Courtesy Jim Smith.

have to be moving in the machine, and the shortest way to move fish would be side on as a fish is longer than the side measurement. Jim decided to make a V-shaped box, and the small fish would lie at the bottom of the 'V' and the larger fish farther up the 'V'. This way they would all be centralised and laid belly up. Then Jim had to think what kind of blade would open and gut the fish, and have the blade adjusted to rise and fall with the varying fish sizes also what kind of rotary brushes would be required to clean out the fish. In Jim's thoughts it was all a matter of trial and error. After a lot of thought about the various possibilities, it all seemed to fall into place in Jim's mind. The 'V' parts were on an endless belt, with the fish all laid on belly up. After a lot of work the various parts would soon be put together, and after some adjustments the gutting machine was ready for a test run.

Gutting machine. Courtesy Jim Smith.

The Gutting Machine

The White Fish Authority got to hear about this man in Scalloway who was making a machine to gut fish, and their interest was aroused and engineers sent to Scalloway to see what was happening. They looked at the finished machine and were very impressed with what they saw. Would it now be possible, they wondered, to get a trial for the machine on a fishing boat and see how it would behave in real working conditions at sea? Willie Goodlad, skipper of the *Responsive* LK 37, very kindly agreed to take the machine on board and give it a trial. When it was fitted in the boat and was ready to go to sea, engineers from the White Fish Authority came to Scalloway and accompanied the *Responsive* to see the machine working. It all worked just as Jim had envisaged; fish were gutted and the rotary brushes cleaned out the fish, with water running through the machine all the time.

The fish were coming in all sizes, some with big heads and longer bodies, and some fatter than others, so how would the blade cope with that? Jim said that difficulty was surmounted by a simple cam in the machine, which adjusted the blade to the size of the fish lying in the 'V'. The engineers tried to fool the machine by putting in some small fish followed by various sizes of larger fish.

M/B **Responsive.** *Inset: Willie Goodlad. Photos: Clement J. Williamson*

The machine could not be fooled however, always setting the blade correctly to the size of the fish.

The engineers were very enthusiastic and decided to take the machine to the industrial development unit in Hull. There, some of the parts were machined more finely. Then there were more tests on boats and it was rated a huge success.

Jim applied to get a patent for the machine and this was obtained without any difficulty. Then an engineering firm, C. F. Wilson from Aberdeen, wanted to manufacture the 'fish gutting machine' and hundreds were made and sold on to fishing boats. I can only repeat, and I am sure you will agree with me (and Bobby Fraser), that Jim Smith MBE from Berry Farm is a very clever man.

DA RUNDSTYKKE AFFAIR

Bertie and the Standard 10. Photo: Willie Smith

DID I TELL YOU about the visit Bertie and I made to Sumba with the dear little 1934 Standard 10? We were visiting the island of Suduroy, the southernmost isle in the Faroe group, and were staying in Tvoroyri, situated near the middle of the island. On this particular day, the weather was misty and dull but we decided to go and see the lighthouse at Sumba (the equivalent of our Sumburgh). After breakfast, we set off to the south end of the isle, stopping in the various villages and taking time to look around, as we were on holiday. We were delayed for about 20 minutes by roadmen repairing a single track road, which made us feel at home! Near the south end of the island we drove through two tunnels, one of which was about two kilometres long. The mist had really settled in by the time we arrived at Sumba and all we could see were some houses and a bit of the shoreline. The lighthouse was about another two miles farther south but was not visible, so we decided to give it a miss.

Twisting roads. Photo: Willie Smith

Steep roads in Faroe. Photo: Willie Smith

After exploring the side roads and looking around, the time had crept up to midday and we were starting to think that a cup of tea or coffee and something to eat would go down nicely. It seemed quite a while since breakfast. We had eaten corn flakes every morning at breakfast; it did not matter where in Faroe we stayed, they always served corn flakes for the first course at breakfast. One morning, as Bertie was pouring milk on his plate of flakes, he looked up and said, "Willie, does du ken dis."

I said, "No, I dunna, whit is hit?"

He looked at me seriously and said, "I don't think I will ever be able tae look a corn flake in the face again."

Now, just like two growing boys, we were feeling the pangs of hunger. Rounding a corner, we saw on a building the magic word CAFÉ. Just the job, we thought; tea and coffee at last. Bertie pulled into the side of the road and I went to see if they were open. I had a choice of three doors facing me so I tried the door on the left. It was locked, as was the middle door, but the right hand door opened to my touch. I walked in expecting to see tables, chairs, cups and plates, but found myself in someone's living room. I could hear voices, so I beat a hasty retreat. Back in the car, I said to Bertie, "Drive on quickly," and then broke the sad news that there would be no tea and peerie cakes just yet.

Further along, we saw a shop and thought we would get something to eat there, even if it was a tin of sardines or bully beef. Bertie stopped the car and we walked in the shop door. There was an attractive teenage girl behind the counter, and six or seven people walking around with baskets and message lines. The sudden appearance of two foreign looking septuagenarians put an end to thoughts of messages – all eyes and interest were now focused firmly on us.

Bertie stepped up to the counter and said to the girl, "Have you any rolls?"

She looked at him blankly, so Bertie tried again. "Rolls, you know what rolls are, don't you?"

Still wearing a blank look, she shrugged her shoulders and there were mutterings from the shoppers, as no one could speak English.

I can speak a little Norwegian, and as the Faroese seemed to understand my attempts, I went up to the counter and the poor girl likely wondered what this other foreigner was going to say. I said in Norwegian, "Har du noen rundstykke?" (Have you any rolls?)

The atmosphere in the shop changed instantly, the girl smiled and said, "Ja, ja, rundstykke, ja."

95

Bertie at shop. Photo: Willie Smith

The customers smiled and we were nearly all friends already! The girl then came from behind the counter and pointed to a shelf on which lay bags of rolls and loaves of bread. I selected a bag with four rolls and brought it to the counter.

Bertie said, "We will need something to go on the rolls."

Once more I tried some Norwegian, and all I could think to say was, "Har du spekeskinke?" (Have you smoked ham?)

This time the girl went to a large fridge. She opened the door and there were packets of all kinds of cooked meats, all the way from Denmark. I took a packet of ham and brought it to the counter. I then asked the girl for, "To flaske ol." (Two bottles of beer.)

"Boy," Bertie said, "what is du wanting oil for?"

When she set two bottles of Foroya Bjor Pilsnar beer on the counter, all he said was, "Ah hah!"

Then I asked, "Hva koster det?"

Bertie had a handful of krone notes and paid the girl. While she was ringing up the till and getting change, Bertie turned to me and said, "Willie, I'm awful blyde du's here, boy."

Da Rundstykke Affair

When we left the shop there were smiles all round. The girl and all the shoppers came out to see us off. We got in the car, Bertie started the engine and, moving off, tooted the horn. We smiled and waved, and they all smiled and waved furiously, but whether they were glad to see us go, or glad that we had been, we'll never know.

We went along the road a bit and saw a little harbour and a pier, so Bertie drove down the road and stopped so we could eat our rolls and drink the Foroya Pilsnar. On the way we passed some men looking at a boat. Two cars were parked there as well and after a while, the men seemed to be going but one of the cars came and parked alongside us. The driver lowered his window, and Bertie did likewise. The man spoke, and with a Faroese 'Shetland' accent said, "Weel boys, how are you da day?"

Bertie said we were fine, then added, "Hold on a moment, I have seen you somewhere before."

"Most likely," the man said, "I used to work in Bolt's Garage in Lerwick and I recognised dy peerie car."

In Faroe. Photo: Willie Smith

THE OLD SMIDDY

AT THE SOUTH END of New Street, on the seaward side, was the Old Smiddy. This blacksmith's shop was established by Laurence Mowat, a Scalloway man. He had learned his trade with a blacksmith by the name of Gellie, who worked in Lerwick. The business was carried on by Laurence's son, George Mowat, and later still by his grandson, also Laurence Mowat. The Old Smiddy is still standing although many years have passed since the ring of hammer on anvil was heard beating out spade and tushkars.

My brother-in-law Clement and Laurence were great friends and this is a yarn related to me by Clement. Laurence always contended that the Old Smiddy or the area close by was haunted. While working with his uncle, George, they had on various occasions heard footsteps coming down the steps from the road and along to where there was a large flat stone slab outside the door. The footsteps would stop there and march as if marking time. Laurence said he was determined to find what it was that came down the steps and stopped outside the door.

One night when they heard the footsteps, Laurence positioned himself at the door with his hand on the latch. The footsteps tramped along to the door and began marching on the stone slab. Laurence flung open the door, but there was nobody there and nothing to be seen. All was silent and the moon was shining across the harbour.

Clement asked Laurence what his uncle thought about it all. "He did not say very much about it," Laurence said, "only when he heard the footsteps he would say, 'Aye aye, they've come again, come again,' that was all." So the mystery of the footsteps remained.

One night, about half past ten, Clement was walking along the street on his way home. It was a dark night with a fine drizzle falling. The Smiddy had skylights on the nearly-flat roof and if the fire was burning bright and the chimney was smoking and the Tilley lamp glowing, one could see the glare in the drizzle. As Clement came along the street he saw the glare from the skylights and thought, "Goodness me, Laurence is working late tonight, I'll pop in for a yarn before bedtime."

The Old Smiddy

Laurence makes a tushkar with Tammie Henry. Photo: Clement J. Williamson

Laurence Mowat at the Old Smiddy door. Photo: Clement J. Williamson

Clement went down the steps and around towards the Smiddy door, but the place was all in darkness, there was nobody there, no lights, and the door was keyed. Rain was dripping off the roof and the atmosphere was very eerie. He quickly hurried back up to the street and home.

While Clement had not heard anything, quite a few of the neighbours had, at different times, heard the clang of the hammer on the anvil late at night. He made his way home with the very strong impression that he had definitely seen the glare from the skylights. He had also been sure that the Smiddy was occupied and that Laurence had been working there.

That was the only time that Clement ever experienced any uncomfortable feelings about the place, but he had to agree with Laurence, there was something very peculiar associated with the Old Smiddy.

WATER CONNECTING

IN THE 1920s, the houses in Scalloway did not have running water, or bathrooms. All the water needed had to be carried in and when finished with had to be carried out again. There was no mains water running through the village but there were plenty of wells. We stayed in Nicolson's House and our folk got their drinking water from the Lord's Well, which was on the beach where the Prince Olaf slipway is. It was lovely clear water from limestone rocks. The water used for washing was collected rainwater.

In the 1920s and '30s mains water arrived in the village, piped from Njugals Water loch, and a sewage system was laid at the same time. My father fitted up a sink in our upstair flat, and a flush toilet in a shed at the back of the house, so we felt quite modern. Soon, lots of houses wanted a sink with running water, so that provided

The big cut. This trench had to be cut at the top of the Scord to get the water from Njugals Water to the reservoir. The height of the reservoir explains the pressure on the water piped at Main Street. Photo: Clement J. Williamson

WATER CONNECTING

work for my father's firm. Geordie Nicolson, a first class joiner and self-taught plumber, made all the connections.

Nicolson & Co. wanted a sink fitted in the back shop so Geordie and Uncle Robbie were sent to do the work. First they had to dig a hole in the road and find the water main, then dig a track for the lead pipe to enter the building and for the sewer to take the waste away. The water main was fairly deep and the hole had to be big enough to enable Geordie to work at making the connection and soldering the lead pipe to the main. This was done and a large heap of earth was now piled up on one side of the road. Then Uncle Robbie made a wooden stand for the sink to sit on, Geordie fitted a tap, and the lead pipe was laid in the track. All seemed to be going well.

George Nicolson. Photo: Willie Smith

When the time came to connect to the main, Geordie took the water key and turned off the supply at the stopcock. However, instead off removing the key from the stopcock he left it attached. Then he climbed down into the hole while Uncle Robbie went

103

to the workshop to fetch some screw nails to fix the tap in place. When Uncle Robbie came back and saw the water key attached to the stopcock and no sign of Geordie, he thought he would remove it in case someone interfered with it. But instead of pulling it straight out, something (as he said later) made him give the key a half turn. The mains pressure water then shot out of the half-inch hole in the main pipe towards the unsuspecting Geordie.

Down in the hole, Geordie was cleaning the main pipe ready to make the connection when, in his own words, "I heard a kinda whistling sound and then a half-inch jet of water hit me in the chest. Man, it nearly lifted me out of the hole."

Uncle Robbie.
Photo: Clement J. Williamson

He said a few words he was not in the habit of saying as he scrambled to get out of the hole with the jet of water shooting up one leg of his trousers. Soaking wet, he now managed to get to his feet out of range of the water, to see Uncle Robbie doubling up with laughter as he turned off the stopcock. "Robbie, just what the hell is du playing at?" he said.

Uncle could give no explanation apart from a mild "Geordie, I don't know what possessed me."

Geordie's reply, as he headed up the brae for home to get dry clothes, was "Humph."

I had not long been an apprentice joiner, and was working in the workshop with Geordie one day, when an old lady who lived along the street sent word that her kitchen tap needed a new washer. My brother, the boss, asked Geordie to go and fit the washer, but as Geordie and the lady had previously had a disagreement about

Water Connecting

something, he said, "A fine peerie job for Willie. He could easily fit a washer."

I said eagerly, "Yes, I will go, but Geordie must first tell me what to do."

So I got a crash course on how to fit a washer and set off for the old lady's house. When I got there I realised I would have to turn off the water, so I said to the lady I would have to go and find a water key.

"No, no," she said. "There's no need for that. Just take the tap off and I will hold a towel so as to keep the water in the sink."

So, off came the tap and on went the towel, and out came the water – the house was on the main street, the lowest point in the village and where the water pressure was greatest – no towel could keep the water in the sink!

My sleeves were soaking wet, as was the front of my dungarees and the old lady's overalls. The water was running down the back of the sink and coming out over the floor. I realised there was no way I was going to get the washer on before the house was flooded, so I said I was going to put the tap back on and go for a water key.

She said that was fine, and took the towel away. When I tried to get the tap back on, the water squirted everywhere, and I mean everywhere. The lady hurriedly backed off and I was beginning to look like Geordie when he climbed out of the hole at Nicolson & Co. Eventually I got the tap on and helped to clean up the mess.

Da Water Works. Photo: Clement J. Williamson

105

Geordie nearly died laughing when I came back to the workshop with my clothes and even my hair dripping water. I did eventually get the washer on and then helped the old lady to mop up. It was what is known as learning the hard way.

I heard a woman say one day she could not understand why some of the Scalloway folk turned on their water tap first thing in the morning, and let the water run for a while before filling the kettle. I was able to supply the answer to that. The initial supply to a house was through a lead pipe from the main, which was an iron pipe. As nearly all the houses had no bathrooms there was no nightly flushing of toilets by those with weak bladders; they had to go elsewhere. The lead pipe which supplied water to the household tap could, in some places, be quite long and the water which lay in the pipe all night would absorb lead particles which were, of course, very poisonous. So the Scalloway folk turned on their taps first thing in the morning and got rid of the lead contaminated water, then filled their kettles.

Very few lead pipes remain now; they are all either copper or plastic. Old habits die hard they say, and I still run the tap first thing in the morning, even though there are toilets being flushed through the night.

THE NIGHT MY FATHER DIED

ETCHED clearly in my memory is the night of 5th March, 1937; the night my father died. I was seven years old at the time. My mother predeceased him, on 5th March, 1931, when I was nearly two, so I have no memory of her. My father was the main part of my life, as he took me around with him and sometimes to his work. I had two older sisters who looked after me and my sister Anna, who was three years older.

We stayed in Nicolson's House, West Shore, in an upstair flat which had three rooms. In the ben room, I shared a bed with my father, while Anna had a little bed to herself. In the but room, which was a living room and kitchen with a sink and running water at the end window, my sister Chrissie had a bed, and in the small third room, my sister Phyllis had a bed. As was usual in those days, we had an outside toilet, which was not ideal on a stormy winter night.

We always had visitors, which was very lightsome. People visited each other's homes in those days as there was no radio and no TV. News and local events were discussed sitting around the warm stove,

The author and his father.

107

stories were told, and many cups of tea were consumed. One of the visitors to our house was Bertie Hughson, a Vidlin man who worked at the South Setter farm, and a great friend of my father. He would cycle from South Setter once or twice a week and the two of them would sit talking at the open fire in the ben room of an evening. When I went to bed the sound of their speaking never bothered me. Rather, I found it comforting, especially on a winter night, and I was soon fast asleep.

On the evening of 5th March, 1937, my father had gone to the ben room after tea to sit and read. Sometime after seven, Chrissie took me to the sink to have my face washed before I went to bed. Bertie arrived as this was happening and stood and spoke for a few minutes then went through the lobby to sit and talk with father.

My face was all wet and soapy when suddenly Bertie came back in and said, "Your father is not well."

I ran to the door, dodging Bertie, and through the lobby and into the ben room to see my father sitting on the floor at his chair. The others rushed through after me and I was quickly hauled away. That image, clear in my memory, has stayed with me all these years.

Someone rushed off to call Dr Durham, neighbours came in, and Anna and I were told to run down to Aggie Leebie who stayed in the room below our but room. Anna took my hand and we ran down the stair and around the front of the house and in Aggie's door. I was crying. Anna told what had happened, and Aggie took us to sit close by her No. 7 stove.

Some men who were visiting Aggie went upstairs to see if they could help and Aggie made us tea. I remember shaking so much that I could hardly hold the cup. It seemed a long time before someone came to take Anna and myself back up. We were told that Dr Durham had been and that father had had a stroke. When we got upstairs it seemed that the room was full of people. The only person I can recall, apart from my sisters, was Basil Grant who stayed opposite Aggie. Anna and I were put to bed in the but room. When I woke in the morning it was to see white sheets on both windows. It was the custom in those days to blind the windows when there was a death in the house.

The Night My Father Died

I knew something terrible had happened. Dad was nowhere to be seen, and I was confined to the kitchen. My two older sisters were very tearful but not talking. Folk visited but I don't remember being spoken to, although maybe some spoke to Anna. How was a seven-year-old supposed to know what was going on? I don't remember asking any questions but I remember feeling very frightened and cold. The only bright spot in the day for me was when another older sister, Mary, and her husband Clement Williamson visited. Clement talked with me and quietly told a few stories.

Days passed slowly and we had a steady stream of visitors. My pal Connie from next door would visit to keep me company, but we had to be very quiet. Men who had chatted and laughed before were now very sombre and spoke in hushed tones, and the women were tearful. The day of the funeral arrived and it was held at our house. Many men came and shook hands with everyone, myself included, but the only man I have a definite memory of was the Baptist minister from Burra Isle, the Rev. William Isbister, perhaps because he smiled and spoke to me. Hymns were sung and prayers said and then there was the viewing of the remains, which I did not understand. Clement asked me if I

Agnes Thomson, aka Aggie Leebie.

Mary and Clement, 1930s.

The author and Connie. Photos: Clement J. Williamson

wanted to view, but I declined, as I did not know what was going on, apart from it having something to do with my dad being ill and not being seen for days. After the viewing there was a lot of activity, the men all left, then there was the noise of many feet moving in the road outside the house. That gradually faded away and then there seemed an awful silence. Someone had given me an old clock to play with and I worked with it all through the funeral.

The Night My Father Died

The day after the funeral the white blinds on the windows were lifted by a half and the next day were removed completely. I can remember a feeling of relief and hoping things would get back to normal, but of course they never could. A day or so after this there was the washing with Dettol disinfectant, the smell of which I have detested all through my life as it brings back the memory of March 1937. It was the custom then after a funeral that the house and furniture had to be washed all over. It probably was something of a therapy to take minds off losing a loved one, as there was no counselling for adults or children in those far off pre-social work days.

A few more days passed after the funeral, then it was back to school for Anna and myself. I remember being very carefully informed by a group of older boys that my father was dead and I would never see him again. I did not tell anyone what the boys had said, so next day my older sisters could not understand my reluctance to go to school. Children can be very cruel without meaning to be so.

A STORY FROM 1920

Ladysmith and Howarth's Yard. Photo: Clement J. Williamson

AS A PRE-SCHOOLBOY, a schoolboy, a teenager and a young man I visited my grandparents' house at Ladysmith, Scalloway, one of a row of little cottages built on the side of the Gallow Hill. The two main rooms were fairly large and it was fashionable at the time to have large pictures on the walls. There were many pictures in the but room. All the pictures were of family and close relatives except one, which had a lot of writing on it. I remember asking Granny who the people in the pictures were. Granny, always patient, would tell me names, so in time I felt I knew them. When the time came that I could read easily, I got interested in the picture with writing. It was a framed parchment about saving human lives and my grandfather's name, Thomas Umphray, was on it.

Another house in Scalloway I used to visit at that time was the house of James Wishart at Kirk Park. On a wall in his house was a similar parchment, with the name James Wishart on it. To my young mind this was puzzling. How did James Wishart have a parchment with his name, the same as my grandfather had?

A Story From 1920

Framed parchment hangs on the little cottage wall. Photo: Willie Smith

    I asked Granny about this and she told me the story of how, on a stormy winter's night many years ago, five men from Scalloway saved the lives of 17 men, women and children from Burra Isle. Of course, as children do, I had to have the story repeated to me many times. Many years have passed since I was a schoolboy and my memory of the story, though not forgotten, was much dimmed.

WILLIE'S TALES & TRAVELS

That is, until a few months ago. In an idle moment I was browsing through some old cassette tapes. Suddenly from one came the voice of my uncle, Lowrie Umphray, recounting this same story.

About 4pm on 31st December, 1920, the motor boat *Welfare* LK 228, owned by Davie Pottinger, was brought from anchor in the East Voe to Blacksness Pier. The boat then left Scalloway for Mid Isle, Burra, a distance of four miles or so, with 17 people on board: seven women and children and ten men. Some of them had been to Lerwick on business, while others had been making purchases for the New Year. Among them were the Rev. H. Reeves, Baptist Church minister, and Mr John Little, schoolmaster, with his wife and two young girls.

The wind was from the south-east and blowing hard. Outside Scalloway harbour the *Welfare's* engine stopped and, in spite of the men's efforts, could not be restarted. (It was rumoured that someone had helped himself to the fuel.) The men aboard cast an anchor, but by then the wind had increased to near gale conditions and the anchor would not hold. Luckily, a small Shetland model boat was being towed astern and some of the men got the small boat alongside and boarded. They rowed, with great difficulty, about 100 yards or so to a point of land somewhere near Punds Voe, and a crofter-fisherman leapt ashore and hurried along the coast towards Scalloway.

The men rowed back to the *Welfare*. By this time it was very dark, which made it impossible to try to land women and children. A storm lantern was lit to alert any boat that might come to their rescue. They could do nothing now but wait. The minister and the schoolmaster told stories and cheered up the women and children. The *Welfare* continued to drag her anchor but finally held on a shoal off Langa.

Meanwhile, the crofter-fisherman had made it along the banks broo to Scalloway and told his story at Nicolson & Co.'s shop.

It was teatime in the little cottage on the side of the hill and Grandaa, Granny, and their family were all gathered around the table. The No. 7 stove made the room fine and warm but outside it was raining hard and a gale was blowing. Suddenly the door opened so forcefully they thought it had blown open, but it was a young lad,

A Story From 1920

Little cottage on the side of the hill. Photo: Clement J. Williamson

Jim Cromarty, who worked for Nicolson & Co. As he stepped into the room he paused a moment to get his breath, then looking at Grandaa he said, "The motor boat *Welfare* has broken down and is being driven towards Langa, can you come?"

Grandaa rose from the table and, pausing only to find his cap, disappeared out the door, still with his smucks on his feet.

Five men were called that day to help with the rescue. They were: William Slater, aged 59; Bobby Slater, aged 28; James Wishart, aged 44; Thomas Umphray (Grandaa), aged 59; and Laurence Laurenson, aged 39. They met at Nicolson's and had a discussion, then decided to take William Slater's boat, the *Thetis* LK 369, built on the Isle of Papa by William Slater. (Some years later she was sold and renamed *Harvest Gleaner* LK 21.)

She was smaller than Grandaa's boat, the *Surprise*, but of all the boats in the fleet her engine could be started quickest and this would save time. (The *Surprise* had a Gardner engine; the cylinder had to be heated with a blowlamp and it could take up to an hour to get the engine started.)

The men launched a small boat at the west beach and rowed out to the *Thetis*. When they were ready to go, they left a light – a candle lantern – in the small boat at the moorings, so they would find it again in the dark.

As Lowrie was a young boy he could not go out so went to the window. They still had heavy blackout curtains on the window, the same as the kind from the wartime, so Lowrie went behind them and kept the family advised as to what he could see, which was very little. He watched for a light from the boat and after about ten minutes a light appeared in the harbour. He realised it was not where his father's boat was anchored but was puzzled as to why the light never moved. It was, of course, the light in the small boat at the *Thetis*' moorings.

A considerable time passed before the light went out, and after a further 20 minutes or so, Grandaa came back to the house.

The *Thetis* had, after some searching, found the *Welfare*, and managed to get a rope aboard and come alongside. The women and children were brought up from below and some of them scrambled aboard the *Thetis* with the help of the crew. Then the rope broke and the manoeuvring had to start all over again. The *Thetis* came round again and this time all the remaining managed to leap aboard, the youngest being caught by the able-bodied crew.

The journey back to Scalloway was rough and, with the extra people aboard, more dangerous, but they arrived safely at Blacksness. Local people took in the wet and storm-tossed passengers and they were all well looked after. They had nothing but praise for the *Thetis* and her brave crew.

Next morning the *Sylvanus* from Burra, skipper John W. Pottinger, found the anchored, abandoned *Welfare* none the worse, and towed her to Scalloway.

On 30th April, 1921, all five rescuers received word to come to the Scalloway Hotel. There they were each presented with an honorary certificate and ten pounds, a small fortune in those days.

Grandaa's parchment reads: 'The Carnegie Hero Trust Fund. Presented By The Trustees In Recognition Of Endeavour To

A Story From 1920

Save Human Life To Thomas Umphray. Scalloway Shetland, 31st December 1920. Signed by Chairman and Secretary, at Dunfermline 26th April 1921'.

Today, as I write this, the little cottage on the side of the hill stands silent and empty. The walls are bare, no family pictures, and for the first time in 84 years, no framed parchment. The people who lived there are no more, but their memory lingers on. Further along the side of the hill stands my house, and in the hallway, in pride of place, hangs Grandaa's framed parchment.

Footnote: The little cottage has now been given a new look. It is now a very modern little house and is alive and well.

MORE ON DA PRIVY

THE PRIVY at Blacksness, like the other privies along the shore, was built out over the high water mark so that it was self-flushing, and was primarily for the use of the fish curers and herring gutters who worked and stayed in the surrounding area. With an easterly wind any small degree of comfort vanished. It was a case of drop it and run!

As I remember the privy, there were three cubicles which gave each participant a small measure of privacy. At the north end of the building was a separate door which led to the ladies' compartment. At that time there were no gutters staying in the huts so the ladies' end remained locked.

Some people can train themselves to have a bowel evacuation at a set time every day, but one elderly gentleman was so exceptionally regular that it was said the locals used his appearance to set their clocks. On one occasion, some youths who were aware of this decided to play a joke on him, but this had to be done when the sea was under the privy. In preparation for the joke one of their

Gutters and gutters' hut, Blacksness. Photo: Clement J. Williamson

More On Da Privy

Old lady knitting. Photo: Clement J. Williamson

Ploughing match at East Park, 1938. Photo: Clement J. Williamson

number went to Andrew Johnson's east park where swede neeps (turnips) grew. The youth picked a large one, topped and tailed it, and in the long grass cleaned all the earth off. With the neep under his jacket, he returned to the privy area and hid it under the end of the gutters' hut.

When the elderly gent's time of arrival coincided with a high tide, the youths gathered and hid at the back of the huts. Spot on time, the gent appeared and entered the privy. When it was estimated he was in the appropriate position, the youth picked to perform the joke entered the privy with the neep under his jacket and positioned himself in a cubicle. The other boys now crept quietly to the side of the privy and waited. Apart from a brief, "Ay-Ay," no conversation took place inside the privy.

The young man started making grunting, stunking and moaning sounds, always getting a bit louder until, with an extra loud moan, he dropped the neep. The neep hit the water with an almighty splash, to the delight of the boys gathered outside the privy. The young man then gave a satisfied groan, and the elderly gent was heard to exclaim, "Dear God."

More On Da Privy

The prank had gone exactly as planned, and the assembled crowd howled with laughter as the young neep-dropper ran out, followed by all sorts of imprecations from a very indignant elderly gentleman who now realised what had been going on.

Another privy tale goes back to before the war. At the east end of the West Shore beach stood a self-flushing privy; self-flushing because the sea would come right in underneath. This also made it very uncomfortable with a gale from south-south-east. There were no toilets in folk's houses so men were very glad to use it.

Two eight-year-old boys (I was one of them) and a seven-year-old girl always played together. A favourite place was the beach at West Shore where there was always something to interest young minds. When it was an ebb tide there were little crabs and shells to collect, but never did we go near the privy area. On one occasion, when the tide was far out, we had a lot more beach to walk on, and as we walked along suddenly we realised we were way out beyond the privy. Looking back, we saw a strange sight. In one of the privy cubicles, which was now very open to us, was a large white looking object. What it was we could not quite fathom and we started to speak about it. Suddenly, an upside down face appeared and a well-known local voice said, "Whit ta hell are you looking at? Clear off."

Suddenly it dawned on us what the strange looking object was; it was a large bare bum. We started to laugh and giggle and soon the face appeared again, "Go on, bugger off."

So we did, but next day when we saw the owner of the voice on the street it was all laughter again.

MAL DE MER
(Spewing)

IN THE 1950s, the firm of Thomas Smith & Son built houses in Burra Isle for the Zetland County Council. At that time there were no bridges so concrete blocks, sand, slates, wood, workmen and all the necessary sundries had to be ferried by sea. This was done by Hance Smith and Andrew Henry with the ferry boat *Tirrick*, and by William Cecil Leask with the cargo boat *Ord*.

During the years we travelled to Burra Isle on the *Tirrick* we had a lot of fun playing '500'. It got very competitive and sometimes a little bad feeling would creep in until a good hand restored everything. There were two of our men who were always up to playing tricks, and everybody else was fair game. One day they decided to rig a pack of cards. This trick was aimed at a certain man who thought himself a very astute player, and they planned to bring him down with an enormous dunt, and they did.

The rigged pack was kept until he was in the right position for the trick to work. When, one morning, the right occasion arose, the rigged pack was produced and the cards dealt. The cards he picked up were just right for hearts, no trumps with ace high, except that

M/B Tirrick. *Photo: Clement J. Williamson*

Mal De Mer

Hancie at Tirrick's *wheel. Photo: Willie Smith*

WILLIE'S TALES & TRAVELS

Loading the Ord. *Photo: Clement J. Williamson*

Mal De Mer

The Ord *fully laden. Photo: Clement J. Williamson*

he had no joker. It was too good to pass, and the joker might be in the kitty. When he announced seven no trumps, one of the others started to hmm and haaa and said, "I wonder, maybe I should, I think I will. Well, you never know what's in the kitty, do you?"

At that, the about-to-be-tricked man could contain himself no longer. "I'll go the grand slam, I will," he said.

"Well, well then, carry on," said the other.

So the kitty was picked up and there was one ace but no joker. So now he had two aces and hopefully his partner had the joker. It was his play, so he played the ace of hearts, but was promptly trumped by an opponent with the joker (usually when the joker was played there were loud cheers) who continued with a good suit of clubs and took every trick!

It was said that the poor man's face got so red you could feel the heat. On the return trip at night he stayed up on deck.

One rather blustery morning we were gathered at Blacksness Pier waiting the arrival of the *Tirrick* when the firm's lorry arrived with four staircases. The stair for a house had two flights with a half landing. They were fabricated in the workshop at Scalloway and usually transported to Burra with the *Ord*. On this particular occasion we needed staircases in a hurry, so Hancie agreed to

125

Joiners and plumbers at Hamnavoe houses. From left – back row: John Cheyne, Alistair Walter, Jim Thomson, the author. Front: Ian Smith, Tommy Isbister, Jeck Hutchison. Photo: Willie Smith

transport them on the *Tirrick*. We put them on top of the cabin and secured them with ropes, or so we thought.

There were always passengers as well as workmen on the *Tirrick* and this morning two well-dressed men took a seat in the aft end of the cabin. There were no Berghaus fleece jackets and cargo trousers with every pocket stuffed full then; men wore nice suits and overcoats, and these gents were appropriately dressed. We all got seated and out came the cards for the 500. The cards were shuffled and dealt, and then we were on our way.

There were eight men in the forward cabin, and four in the aft cabin playing 500, with the two gents seated right aft. They were on a Shetland holiday and going for a day visit to friends in Hamnavoe. The *Tirrick* had a large wheelhouse so some workmen were in there yarning with Hancie and Andrew. It was rather choppy, so Hancie decided to go to the north side of the Green Holm. When we got by the Holm we got the full blast of the south-west wind and the *Tirrick* heaved about a bit. Suddenly there was a crash and we realised the staircases were moving. Hancie eased the engine as we all rushed for the hatch. The staircases were repositioned and more ropes lashed on, but the staircases had nothing to tie a rope to so their position on the cabin roof was quite precarious. The *Tirrick* was still heaving about some so a few of us stayed in the wheelhouse to keep an eye on the cargo as we headed for Hamnavoe, while the others went back down in the cabin.

A tractor for transport to Burra. Photo: Clement J. Williamson

Madge and Tirrick at Blacksness. Photo: Clement J. Williamson

Willie and Ertie Inkster on Madge. *Photo: Clement J. Williamson*

With the bow of the *Tirrick* diving into the waves and sea washing over the wheelhouse, we could now and then hear cheers and loud noises coming from the cabin down below. Somebody remarked that the joker was surely doing the rounds. When the boat was tied up at the Hamnavoe pier, we started to get the staircases ashore when someone remarked to one of the men from the cabin that, judging from the noise we had heard, the joker had been having a great time.

Mal De Mer

"That was no joker noise," he said. "It was one of the tourists being sick, and the bugger had eaten bacon and egg for his breakfast and now it's all over himself and the cabin floor. Wait until Hancie sees it."

We got the staircases ashore, and were waiting for Lennie to get the lorry when one of the gents appeared up the hatch and asked if someone could help him to get his friend ashore. The two men nearest went and helped to take the sick man ashore and to his friend's house. The poor man, whose legs had turned to rubber, had to be put to bed. He only got back to Lerwick the day after. Oh yes, those were the days.

BERTIE AND WILLIE ON DALSNIBBA

IN AUGUST 1996, my old friend Bertie Jamieson from Melby (I call him my old friend because he is six months older than I am) and I had a mountaineering adventure in Norway. It's true you know, and it happened like this. As the *St Clair* was doing weekend trips to Norway, the Shetland Classic Car Club decided to tour part of the Norwegian west coast. Five car owners signed up for the trip: Graham Johnston with his MG F sports car; George Johnson with his Series 2 E-type Jaguar; Geordie Jacobson with his 1980 Reliant Scimitar; Andrew Morrison (who co-organised the trip with Graham) with his 1971 Morris 1000 pick-up; and Bertie's 1934 Standard 10, a lovely car and certainly the oldest. The passengers in the cars were Andrew's son Morris, Jim Sellens, Wilbert Henry, Catherine Jacobson, and myself.

The Standard 10. Photo: Willie Smith

Bertie and Willie on Dalsnibba

We had a very smooth trip on the *St Clair*, a fine ship. We saw oil-rigs and lots of birds diving for fish, and had some very good food, some drams and lots of yarns. It was dark when we arrived in Bergen but, with Andrew leading, we soon found our way to the hostel where we were to spend the night. Next morning, after a buffet breakfast, we set off on our way to Måløy where we stayed for two days. It was when we were on our way to Ålesund that Bertie and I accidentally went mountaineering.

Like Lerwick café. Photo: Willie Smith

It was in the Geiranger Fjord area and when we were coasting downhill Bertie asked me to look how the fuel was doing. Maybe the gauge was not 100 per cent, or maybe it was me or the time of day, or whatever, but my reply was that we had plenty of fuel; the tank was half-full. The downhill gradient came to an end and we started to climb up a long sloping road that led towards Djupvasshytta and on over the mountain, Dalsnibba, reckoned to be Norway's best viewpoint. That was where both Bertie and I thought we were all going, but we were both wrong.

At Djupvasshytta all five cars stopped, just for a break and a look around, not because Geordie's Scimitar was puffing steam. We all

In Norway. Photo: Willie Smith

gathered by the Scimitar, yarned and admired the view, ignoring the steam from the raised bonnet. The tarmac road ahead of us from Djupvasshytta was downhill now as far as the eye could see, and to the left of us was a road going uphill towards Dalsnibba mountain.

After a while, Bertie turned to me and said, "Well, shall we go?"

We got in the Standard 10, Bertie at the wheel, and we turned up the road towards Dalsnibba. We did not notice the others looking at us in utter amazement, wondering what on earth we were doing. The road to Dalsnibba ended at the summit, with a perpendicular drop down the other side of the mountain. Everyone knew that, well didn't they?

In the Standard 10, Bertie and I were talking away as usual, then I said, "I can't understand why this road is not tarmac. It's just a dirt road."

Bertie replied, "Yes, and you will notice it's getting awful steep."

And he was right, there were lots of hairpin bends and it was getting steeper by the minute. The dear little Standard 10 chugged

Car club admires the view in Norway. Photo: Willie Smith

manfully round the bends and onwards and upwards, before suddenly beginning to falter. The engine slowed from a purr to a put-put, and then there was silence. Bertie pulled on the handbrake and we looked at one another. What now we were thinking?

"That's odd," I said, "we have plenty of fuel."

"Yes," replied Bertie, "but not enough. You see, this car has no fuel pump and the petrol reaches the engine by gravity, and look at the angle we are sitting at."

There was fuel in the tank at the back of the car, but none at the front end where it supplied the engine. We surveyed the scene. A good distance below us, the other four cars looked just like little Dinky toys.

Bertie said, "We will just have to go back down. If we could only get the car turned round then the petrol will reach the engine. Anyway, why are the other cars still sitting down there?"

I had no answer.

The others meantime had been watching our progress and noted that we had now stopped. Fearing that we had suffered a mechanical failure, our good friend and organiser Andrew Morrison decided that maybe we needed a lifeline. So, the mountain rescue team swung into action. The Morris pick-up and the MG were to be the rescue vehicles. The Jaguar and the Scimitar would stay down

Bertie at top of Dalsnibba. Photo: Willie Smith

with George and Jim. The crew of the pick-up were Andrew and Catherine in the front, with Geordie and Wilbert in the back. The MG crew were Graham and Morris.

Meanwhile, on the side of the mountain, Bertie and I were considering how best to go about getting the car turned around to face downhill. We were just starting the turn when we heard the distinctive sound of Andrew's 1971 Morris pick-up, closely followed by Graham's MG. There was much pulling of legs (both legs of Bertie and I) and laughter when we were told we were way off course, and there was no through road at Dalsnibba. More laughter followed when 'they' heard about the fuel crisis.

The pick-up, of course had an electric fuel pump, so it was a simple matter for Andrew and Geordie to disconnect the pick-up's fuel pipe and pump some petrol into a can, which was then put in the Standard. Now that our fuel level was up, were we going to turn and go back down? Not a chance. Bertie did some tickling on the carburettor and the dear little old Standard soon burst into life. We were all going to the top to see the view. It was well worth it, as the view was spectacular.

BERTIE AND WILLIE ON DALSNIBBA

Bertie and I have had many a laugh since, when we recall our one and only mountain climb, and being rescued by the resourceful Andrew and the Car Club's mountain rescue team.

Bertie and Standard 10 on Dalsnibba, Norway. Photo: Willie Smith

MORTAR SHELLS

IN 1940 AND 1941, many soldiers did their training back over from the top of the Gallow Hill above Scalloway, and above where Sycamore Avenue is now. A number of regiments trained there, getting themselves fit to fight the dreaded German armies.

They first dug trenches and dugouts, some of which can still be seen today. It must have been tough going on the poor boys as the ground was hard and stony and most of them had probably never seen or used a pick and shovel in their lives before. There was a drill for the pick work, where they had to raise, strike, break and rake, then start all over again. The soldiers fired rifles and machine guns, and ran and dived among the heather and trenches.

Small boys, and sometimes small girls too, would peep over the Gallow Hill dyke and watch, trembling with fear and excitement at this preparation for war. As the war progressed there was less digging and rifle fire, and there were fewer soldiers running through the hills, so the dugouts were abandoned to the small people of the village to play their own war games in.

The soldiers also learned to fire mortars, and one day after they had all gone away we found some mortar shells in a small depression. How did small children know they were mortar shells? That, I cannot tell, but we knew all the same. They measured about nine or 10 inches long and approx two inches in diameter. They were made of bright alloy material and had tail fins. At first we did not touch them but just looked; we had been well-warned not to touch any military equipment. Then we found lots more lying scattered around and eventually someone did pick one up. We found that they were light and obviously empty. They were all practise shells, and so we played at bombs, throwing them around. Just what would have happened if one had been live, I now shudder to think.

I remember one day when, after proudly taking one home, I got a severe telling off and was ordered to take it back to where I found it. What eventually became of all the shells I do not recollect, but perhaps the military removed them out of the way of small people.

Mortar Shells

However, many years later, I was to meet up with a mortar shell again.

Workmen were digging the foundations for an extension to Scalloway Public Hall, at the place where wartime hospital huts and wards had stood. Some school bairns were walking over the site one day at lunchtime and found an object which was oddly-shaped but looked rather interesting. It was about nine or 10 inches long with tail fins, and it was dull and a bit corroded looking, with earth sticking to it. They picked it up, carried it to the school and took it into a classroom. The teacher was not at all happy about it, and got someone to remove it outside. Whoever removed it carried it to the schoolhouse, where it was laid near the schoolhouse door.

I was working in the schoolhouse kitchen that day when I became aware of a lot of voices outside. After a time I opened the door to see what was going on. Outside the door, five or six school staff were standing looking at something to my right. I was amazed, and a little apprehensive, to see a mortar shell lying along the wall.

"Where did that come from?" I asked. When told, I said, "You had better phone the coastguard. That's a mortar shell and it could be live."

A member of the staff replied, "Nonsense, it's a piece of hydraulic equipment."

"I've seen these things before," I said, "on the top of the west hill in the wartime, and you had better believe me, that is a mortar shell."

So someone phoned the Lerwick coastguard and soon two men arrived. After taking a look, they said they were not taking it in their car, and left. A short while later they came back with a Land Rover, in the back of which was a large box of sand. A small hollow was made in the sand, into which the mortar shell was carefully placed and covered. They then left for Lerwick. A bomb disposal crew came to Shetland next day to deal with the shell, and I'm told it made quite a nice little bang at the Greenhead. Better there than in the school!

Not long after this episode, I was clearing a shed for people who were moving house and I found about a dozen or so Oerlikon tracer shells (relics of the Shetland Bus) in a tin box. After the mortar bomb episode I made sure they were given to the right people to dispose off.

Even to this day wartime hardware is still being found in the islands, and goodness knows what harmless looking items folk may have stored in their houses and sheds.

THE SWEDISH CONNECTION

Swedish and Scalloway boats. Photo: Clement J. Williamson

IN THE EARLY 1930s or maybe even earlier, some fishing boats from Bohuslan in Sweden made Scalloway their base for the summer fishing season. What kind of fish they were after I do not know, but in the photos, lines can be seen. I know of two places where the boats came from, Mollosund and Kyrkesund. The boats and the men were a source of interest to the local people, but there was something missing, communication. No one could talk to them, because no one could speak Swedish. They, in turn, could not talk to the locals because none of them could speak English.

One local man decided to change all this. Clement J. Williamson, the local photographer, obtained a copy of Burt's *Swedish-English Dictionary* (now in my possession), published in New York, price one dollar, and he studied this in his spare time. A clever man, he soon memorised all the words he thought might be in everyday use. The correct pronunciation and putting them all together to make a sentence was something that would have to wait till the Swedish boats came back to Scalloway in the summer. Come back they did, and the Swedes were very pleasantly surprised to hear a local man using some of their words.

Clement with Swedes.

THE SWEDISH CONNECTION

Swedes at Blacksness. Photo: Clement J. Williamson

As far as I remember, there were two fishermen who took an interest in furthering Clement's learning of their language, Axel Pettersson from Mollosund, and Josef Jansson from Kyrkesund. Josef was skipper of the fishing boat *Elsey* MD 482. Axel and Josef kept in touch with Clement right up to the time of their deaths.

Josef became a great friend and visited Clement and his wife Mary (my sister) whenever they were in Scalloway. My sister Anna was a little girl at this time and at Christmas she was greatly excited to get a Christmas card from Josef in Sweden. Year after year, he and Anna sent each other a card at Christmas and when, on 9th December, 1986, aged 85 years, Josef died, his wife Edith, who was Norwegian by birth, continued the tradition. When Anna died in 2000, at Christmas time I carried on the tradition and exchanged a card with Edith, until she died in March 2008.

Axel Pettersson died on 3rd January, 1972, aged 80 years. His family kept in touch with Clement for many years. The letter informing Clement of Axel's death was written by a daughter, Anita, and started, "Dear friend of our father".

Clement's command of the Swedish language had become so good that he was now an unofficial interpreter. (Many years after the war a Swedish visitor told Clement that he spoke Swedish like

Josef Jansson. Photo: Clement J. Williamson

The Swedish Connection

Elsey MD 482. Photo: Clement J. Williamson

a Bohus man.) Sometimes the fishermen would need the attention of a dentist or a doctor, and always Clement would have to be present. Some occasions were quite serious, but others could be funny searching for the right word. One day a fisherman came and asked Clement to come to the boat as there was a man ill. Clement discovered the man had abdominal pains so he phoned for Dr Roche. They both went to the boat and climbed down to the cabin where the sick man lay. After an examination by the doctor, and some questions, failed to find anything obvious, Dr Roche asked Clement to find out if the man's bowels had moved that day. This put Clement in a quandary, as he did not know the Swedish word for bowels.

He thought for a while then a word which he thought would be universally known came to him, and he asked the Swede, "Hafva du shit i dag?"

The reply came swift, "Ja ja, tre ganger."

"Well, doctor," Clement remarked, "three times is not bad."

As there did not seem to be anything seriously wrong, some medicine soothing to the innards was administered and the incident was over, except for the laughter going back up the road.

Christmas card to Lille Anna.

THE SWEDISH CONNECTION

The Swedes, when walking the roads at weekends, nearly all wore fancy decorated clogs. The clogs were sharp-pointed and had painted designs. Lots of folk would have liked a pair, but money was always in short supply. A neighbour of Clement's, a carpenter, said he would really like to have a pair. When a Swedish skipper told Clement he would like to get a model sailboat for his son, Clement thought of the carpenter. A pair of Swedish clogs for a model boat. Surely that would be a fair exchange. So the deal was set up, the skipper promised clogs, and the neighbour promised a model boat, with Clement acting as interpreter.

As the winter wore on, Clement would occasionally ask his neighbour how the model boat was getting on. There was always a report – getting the deck on now, making the mast, fitting the rudder, nearly ready for painting – always a good report. The whole village now knew about the model boat, and that a fine pair of Swedish clogs would be arriving in the summer. Lots of folks were envious. People would ask the carpenter how the model boat was progressing and always got a good report. However, no one ever got to see the model boat, and Clement started to feel a little apprehensive about this.

The carpenter with Magnus Wylie at Eshaness Lighthouse. Photo: Willie Smith

Then came the day when the fishing boats were tonking in the harbour towards Blacksness Pier. People went to see them and nodded their heads to men they had nodded to the year before. Clement shook hands and talked with men who were now old friends. Soon, there was the skipper with the clogs, looking for his model boat. However, there was no sign of the carpenter. That weekend, the carpenter seemed to have mysteriously disappeared. He turned up on Monday when the boats were back fishing, and said he had been doing a job in Lerwick.

A few weekends later the skipper questioned Clement. Where was the carpenter, and why did he not show himself with the, as the skipper put it, "leetle shep"?

Clement collared the carpenter next day and demanded to see the model boat. The carpenter had his answer: the boat, he said, was in Lerwick having sails fitted. Being the man who set up the deal, Clement now concluded that there was no model boat, but said nothing.

The weeks went by and all too soon it was the Swedes' last weekend in Scalloway for that year. Clement and the skipper went

The crew of Elsey, *1933. Photo: Clement J. Williamson*

The Swedish Connection

looking for the carpenter. A villager told them he had seen the carpenter going into his workshop, and so there they went. The door was keyed but Clement shouted that they knew he was in there. A very guilty looking carpenter appeared and assured them that the boat was still in Lerwick, and he would get it on Wednesday. The skipper told Clement that they would call in to Scalloway on their way home next Friday morning to collect the leetle shep, and hand over the clogs.

The fishing boat tonked into the harbour on Friday morning and Clement went to the pier, along with other nosey people who, it would seem, had nothing better to do. They all knew about the leetle shep, and wanted to see any fun that might ensue. When the skipper came ashore Clement took his arm and they walked away from the onlookers to where they could not be overheard. Speaking Swedish, of course, Clement told the skipper that the carpenter had been dishonest with them, and that he had no leetle shep, and it would seem had never intended to make any leetle shep. Clement expressed his sorrow about the whole affair and said he was very angry with the carpenter.

All through the conversation he was eye-to-eye with the skipper, whose face was now very grim. He nodded two or three times then told Clement to come aboard the boat with him. Down in the cabin he produced a brown paper parcel, which he opened to reveal a pair of decorated clogs; the clogs for the model boat. He wrapped them up in the paper, and handed them to Clement. "You have them, you tried your best, I give them to you to wear."

Clement was called on many times to help the fishermen. Sometimes he would have to get a taxi and go to Lerwick with them to see the Swedish consul, and act as interpreter as the consul of that time could not speak Swedish. It was something Clement enjoyed doing, as he liked to meet and speak to people.

One night I was at Clement's when there was a furious knocking at the door. Clement was doing something (I don't remember what) and he shouted to me to see who it was. When I opened the door it was a stranger who immediately started to speak in, what turned out to be, Swedish. Not understanding a word, I held up my hand but then caught one word I thought I had heard before. It sounded like "tandklara". I thought, it's a tooth he is talking about, so I pointed to my teeth.

"Ja Ja," was the reply and by this time Clement had come on the scene. A Swedish fishing boat was at Blackness Pier with a crewman needing a dentist and, needless to say, Clement arranged for that to happen.

Over the years I heard many stories, and can still recall one or two.

One day after the war, word came to Scalloway that there was a Swedish seaman in the Gilbert Bain Hospital who could speak no English, and no one at the hospital could speak Swedish. Clement set out for Lerwick. At the hospital he was directed to a bed at the far end of the men's ward. As he walked, he noticed there were screens all round one of the beds. The seaman was very pleased to see him and have someone to talk to. As they talked, they spoke louder and yet louder, and they were laughing too. Suddenly, at the screened bed a white clad figure appeared and, waving his arms above his head, shouted, "Will you stop that bloody noise!"

It was none other than Daniel Lamont, the surgeon.

In May 1984, Swedish Ambassador Leif Liefland and his wife made a visit to Shetland. The Lord Lieutenant of Shetland, Magnus M. Shearer, who was also the Swedish consul, took them for a run to Scalloway. "I would like you to meet an interesting man who stays here," Mr Shearer remarked.

When the ambassador and Clement met, they spoke Swedish. Clement spoke about the times before the war when the Swedish fishing boats spent weekends at Blackness pier. He told about the fishermen, what they did, and what they said. To Clement, the ambassador was just another Swede. Mr Shearer told me Clement had asked Mr Liefland if he had known any of the fishermen. Very diplomatically, the ambassador answered he was not sure if he had known any of them. In a letter to Mr Shearer after the visit, the ambassador asked him to convey to Mr Williamson, "our best regards, and whose perfect Swedish greatly impressed us."

Clement had some bad health in 1993 and had to go to hospital a time or two, visits he would rather have done without. Inspector Arnold Duncan of the local police one day met the honorary

The Swedish Connection

Lief Liefland (left) at The Studio with Clement, Mrs Liefland, Mrs Shearer and Magnus Shearer.

Swedish consul, Mr Magnus Shearer, in Lerwick, and in the course of conversation, Clement's admission to the Gilbert Bain was mentioned. The Swedish connection was discussed and Inspector Duncan wondered to Mr Shearer why Clement had never been recognised for his invaluable work for all the Swedish fishermen who visited Scalloway in pre-war years. Mr Shearer thought about this, and promptly did something about it. He then discovered that Ambassador Lief Liefland, after his visit to Shetland in 1984, had set the ball rolling.

Clement got a letter dated 28th June, 1993, from Lennart Eckerberg, KCMG, Sweden's ambassador in London. He said Clement's services as interpreter had been much appreciated and that he hoped to see him when he visited Shetland next year. Clement was very pleased indeed to get the letter, but was even more pleased to hear from Magnus Shearer that he was to be awarded the Polar Star Medal as an expression of the gratitude of the Swedish state for services over the years. Another letter from

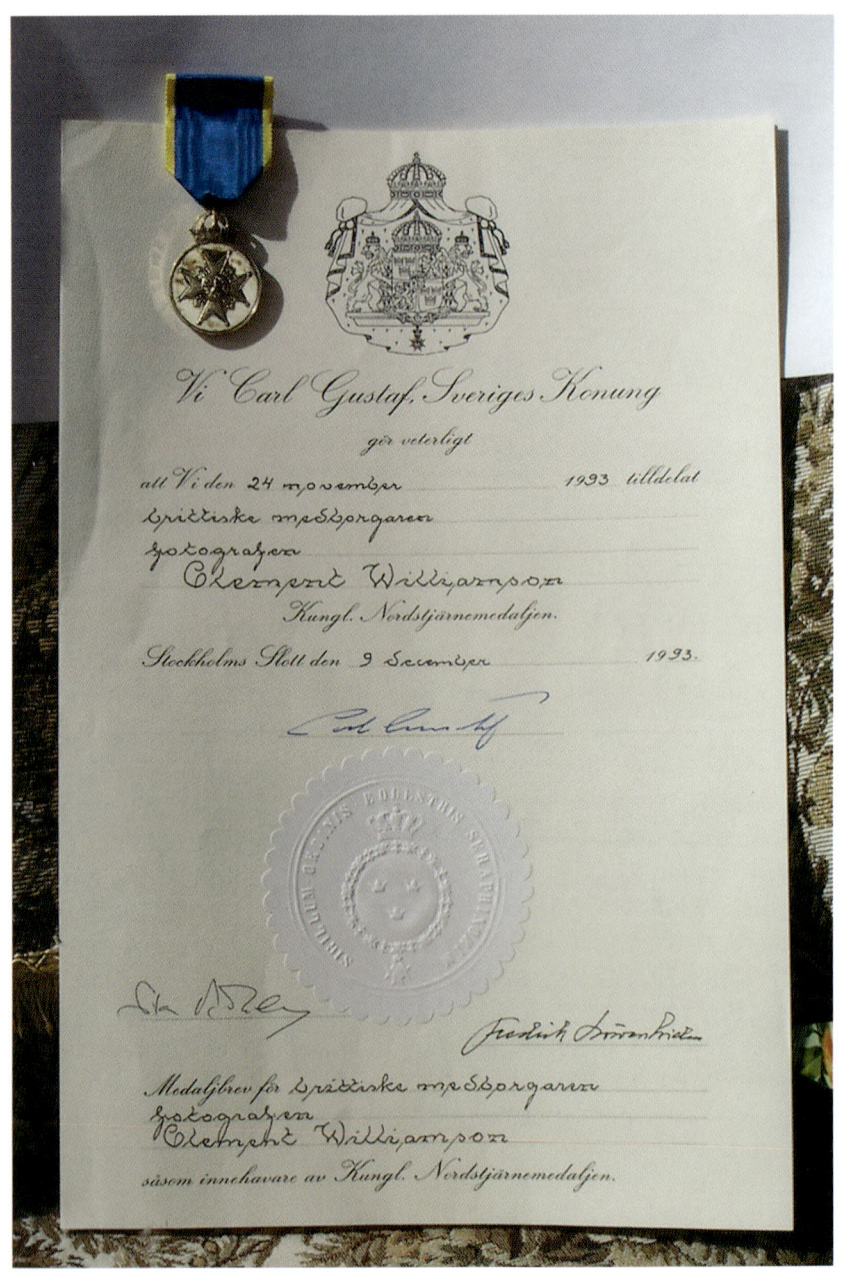

Clement's medal. Photo: Willie Smith

The Swedish Connection

the ambassador dated 7th January, 1994, regretted that he was not able to travel to Shetland to present the medal personally, but he knew that Clement was a worthy recipient.

So it was arranged that Honorary Consul Magnus Shearer would present the medal on behalf of Carl Gustaf, King of Sweden. Unfortunately, Clement was in the Gilbert Bain Hospital and his health was not very good. Alistair Coutts, consultant surgeon at the hospital, arranged for the presentation to be made in ward two. A few relations and friends, with some hospital staff, were there to see the medal being presented by Mr Shearer. As a Lerwick photographer was to be there, very foolishly none of the guests took a camera. The photographer, with an assistant and several cameras took lots of photos, or so we thought. A photograph of the historic event appeared in *The Shetland Times*, but to Clement's and friends' disappointment no other photos were ever forthcoming, despite many enquiries to the photographer. Clement died on 18th April, 1994, aged 90 years.

One of the Swedish fishing boats that used to come in to Scalloway was the *Maud* MD 76, from Kyrkesund. The skipper was Karl Abrahamson. His son, 19-year-old Mauritz Karlsson, was a crew member and they, with others, were known to some of the local people. In July 1935, the *Maud* left Sweden for the Shetland fishing grounds. Prior to leaving, Mauritz had been in contact with measles, and soon it became clear that he was showing signs of the trouble, so he took to his bunk and kept warm. In the cabin it was hot and uncomfortable so one fine night he came up on deck for some fresh air. As he felt good, he stayed up for some while. Next day, he could not be roused and obviously was very ill, so the *Maud* made all speed for Scalloway.

When the *Maud* arrived in the village, a crew member ran to Blacksness House and told Clement Williamson. He went to the post office next door and called Dr Roche. The two of them went aboard the boat, and down to the cabin. Many questions were asked by Dr Roche, and Clement, as interpreter, was kept busy. It was measles and lobar pneumonia said the doctor's report. In spite of all Dr Roche did, young Mauritz, at 6.15am on the sixth day of July, died. It undoubtedly was his stay on deck that had brought on the

WILLIE'S TALES & TRAVELS

Maud *MD76*. Photo: *Clement J. Williamson*

pneumonia. Karl Abrahamson asked Clement to send a telegram to the pastor at Kyrkesund for him to break the news to the family.

The death had to be registered, which Clement attended to with Walter Mowat, registrar, and a coffin had to be made. Uncle Robbie, many years later recalling the event, told me that Mauritz's father walked the street, crying. When he came to the piece of green known as Meggie Ollies green, across from the Eventide Home and near where Uncle Robbie stayed, he flung himself down on the grass crying, uncontrollably. Uncle said it was heartbreaking to see him, and to make matters worse, he said, you could not talk to the man. Uncle Robbie went to the green, sat down beside him, and held his hand for a while. After a time, Karl Abrahmson recovered, and went back to the *Maud*. It was a sad time indeed; prayers were said in the churches and the whole village mourned with Karl Abrahamson on the death of his son.

Meanwhile, in Kyrkesund, the telegram was duly delivered to the house of the pastor. The pastor, however, was away on holiday so the servant girl set the telegram on the mantelpiece, and there it stayed. Several days later the people of Kyrkesund were surprised to hear the tonk-tonk of a boat and to see the *Maud* come steaming in the harbour. Imagine the consternation when they saw her flag flying at half-mast.

People hurried to the pier. What could have happened? Someone had died. One of the older men? What a shock for the family and the folk in Kyrkesund it was when they heard it was 19-year-old Mauritz.

Hearing the story from Clement many times, I always wondered where in Sweden the telegram was received? Was the post office that accepted it a long way from Kyrkesund? Did the person who delivered the telegram know the message it contained? Why did no one mention it to someone? The questions are endless. Bad news travels fast, and this indeed was bad news. The servant girl would not have opened a telegram to the pastor. It was indeed a sad occasion.

In 1995, I decided to join Andrew Morrison's coach tour to Norway and Sweden. When I got the tour papers, my sister Anna saw them and thought she would also go along. The party were to have a

Edith and the author.

day in Gothenborg where we could do as we pleased. As Kyrkesund was somewhere near to Gothenborg, Anna wrote to Edith Jansson (widow of Josef, skipper of *Elsey* MD 482), and said we would try and visit her on that day, a Saturday. Edith sent Anna a photo of her house, so that when we got to Kyrkesund we would find her, and it sounded very easy.

The people at the hotel in Gothenborg were not much help as to how to get to Kyrkesund. I don't think they even knew where it was. We were told to try the bus station. On the Saturday morning at the very busy bus station, we were told after much searching through timetables that we could get on a bus which stopped at Kyrkesund, but that none came back through to Gothenborg that day. If only we had had Edith's phone number a lot of hassle and frustration could have been avoided. So, what were we to do next?

Walking away from the office we saw a taxi rank, and wondered about a taxi to Kyrkesund. There were 12 to 15 taxis, and all the drivers were even more foreign to Sweden than us two from Shetland. I approached the first driver and asked if he spoke English. He did

THE SWEDISH CONNECTION

Kyrkesund, Sweden. Photo: Willie Smith

not, but signalled for me to wait. He came back with an older man who said, "Hallo," but not much more.

I thought I would try some Norwegian, and said, "Hva kosta taxi til Kyrkesund, og vente 30 minuter?" (How much would it cost for a taxi to Kyrkesund and wait for 30 minutes?)

He understood the gist of that, and by this time all the other drivers were gathered round. It was obvious none of them knew where Kyrkesund was, and they all jabbered away for a while, then one of them ran towards his taxi, and the older man signalled for us to wait. The day was wearing on, but the sun was shining, and it was hot, so we waited.

The driver came back with a map which they spread out on the bonnet of the first taxi. After a lot of talk, the older man signed for me to come and look. They had found Kyrkesund. The old one said, "One thousand kroner" (equal to 100 pounds). I just waved my hand and turned away. Quickly, he then said, "OK, eight hundred."

We walked away from them, and Anna spoke, "We will likely never be this way again, it's our one and only chance to see Edith."

Edith's house. Photo: Willie Smith

So we went to a hole in the wall and with a bit of plastic got 800 kroner. Soon, in the most expensive taxi run we had ever had, we were heading out of Gothenborg. The driver had to consult the map several times but eventually we arrived at the little village of Kyrkesund. The taxi stopped in a car parking area and we got out.

I said, "What now, where do we start?"

Just at that moment a woman's voice said, "Anna, lill Anna."

We turned and looked, as a woman appeared at the side of a house. It was Edith, the taxi had stopped right in front of her house.

Edith spoke no English, only Norwegian, but hugged us, and gave us a very warm welcome, and never stopped talking. She had been expecting us. What a disappointment it would have been for her – and us, especially Anna – if we had not taken that taxi. Edith led the way into the house where we saw the table was laid for lunch for five people. Anna and I both spoke some Norwegian, and after getting Edith to slow up a little we managed to convey to her that we were only there for half an hour. That was not going to do at all, one of her sons and his wife were also coming for lunch and to meet us,

The Swedish Connection

The author with Edith and Anna at Josef's grave.

Having tea on the balcony. Photo: Willie Smith

so I was told to go and send the taxi away. I went and paid the taxi driver, thanked him, and told him he was free to go.

It was a great pleasure to meet Edith. Soon her son Leif and his wife Marit arrived. As they both spoke English it made life easier for us. After a very enjoyable lunch they took us for a tour of the area and we visited the graveyard where Josef lay. It was a beautiful day, no wind and really hot, what a change from the Shetland weather. In the evening we had tea on the roof balcony and talked in English and Norwegian. Later in the evening, Leif and Marit drove us back to Gothenborg. The visit to Kyrkesund, and meeting Edith, Leif and Marit, was certainly the highlight of the Norway and Sweden tour.

Marit, Leif, Anna and Edith at Josef's grave. Photo: Willie Smith

303 RIFLE CARTRIDGES

ONE DAY, Douglas Duncan and I were walking home from school along the High Road (now Castle Street), when we saw at the side of the road some 303 cartridges which had been dropped by soldiers on a training exercise. We quickly gathered them up and took them to a shed in the High Road quarry that belonged to Douglas's grandfather, Geordie Cheyne, and hid them in a corner until we could get back to them. We had heard that inside the cartridges were little sticks of some kind of explosive. If these little sticks were laid end to end on a piece of wood and lighted with a match they apparently would not explode, but burn and leave a charred line on the wood. We wanted to try this, but the problem was how to get the little sticks out of the cartridges.

Douglas and Billy. Photo: Clement J. Williamson, courtesy Billy Duncan

Willie's Tales & Travels

There was no hacksaw in the shed or we would have tried sawing them open. However, the face of the quarry had the answer. There were cracks in the stone so we fitted the bullet ends into one of the cracks and then threw stones at the brass cartridges, the idea being to break them in two. Upon reflection, it was a crazy thing to do, but at the time it seemed a good idea and most of the time it worked. We would stand at the corner of the shed, throw a stone and then dodge back, just in case. We did not always hit them but when we did the brass cartridges broke easily and out ran the little sticks.

We collected quite a quantity of little explosive sticks, and found a piece of wood on which to line them up. The next problem was how to get them burning as we had no matches. Douglas, however, knew where his mother kept matches, so he went to the house and took a few, unknown to his mam. We lined up the little sticks, lit an end, and watched them burn with a hissing sound. We were greatly pleased with the burnt lines they made on the wood.

We were now left with the empty brass cases, which we thought should go off with a bang if hit on the cap end. So we set them in the quarry cracks and threw stones, but the cartridges did not go off, which was probably just as well.

REPLENISH AT VEE SKERRIES

THE FOLLOWING STORY of the Burra Isle fishing boat *Replenish's* near-disaster at the Vee Skerries, was told to me by Stanley Pottinger. Stanley was a crew member and a son of the skipper, John L. Pottinger, Rockmount, Hamnavoe.

"I would like to tell you a story about what happened to us in the fishing boat *Replenish*. It was on the morning of the 9th December, 1957. The boat was anchored at Easter Dale, so we left our homes in Hamnavoe between one and two o'clock. In those days we did not have a van, so we walked to Easter Dale beach where we hauled down our small boat and went off to the *Replenish*. This was a fine morning, I think it was a Monday if I mind right, but it was the 9th of December, anyway. As I said, it was a fine morning then and we were going to the Vee Skerries. There had been reports of fish there, and we knew of several other boats going as well – *Northern Light*, *Press On*, to name some. We left Easter Dale and set off for the Vee Skerries. As we were steaming north for the Skerries the wind started to freshen. My late brother, John William, was at the wheel giving our father a break below, as he would take over after a while. As we steamed northwards we were all in our bunks down below, and soon we were aware of the motion of the boat. Coming way down near the Vee Skerries the wind had freshened up so much that the other boats were all turning and going back home.

"John William called up the skipper (father) and told him the weather conditions and that some of the other boats seemed to be heading home. So we just dodged a bit farther north and soon were bewast the Vee Skerries, and then my father came up to the wheelhouse. We dodged for a while longer and then he thought, it's going to be no morning for fishing, so he turned the boat to make for home. The other boats by this time would have been coming up here for about Fuglaness, or nearer Scalloway maybe. Turning, we set off for home, but we had not steamed very far when there came a terrible motion, and we never knew until a great big tidal lump struck us on the starboard side, and laid the boat over on her beam

Replenish with catch. Photo: Clement J. Williamson

ends. Just right on the back of that, another lump struck us and came right in over; right in over and washed away half of the galley and the side of the wheelhouse.

"We were, by this time, all sitting in the galley, except for my father who was in the wheelhouse, and my brother, John William, who had gone down to his bunk to have a nap. The sea washed us all out of the galley and over the side. My father was washed out of the wheelhouse and over the side as well. Our lifeboat had gone over too, but was floating. The whole boat was laid right over and the warps and all were washed out over the side, so that the derrick that we lifted in our fish with was out over the water and had warps hooked all over it. When she half-righted herself again then we could see the ropes hanging from the derrick.

"We were all washed over but my father managed to get hold of a rope and he hauled himself back in over again and the first he did was to get to what was left of the wheelhouse, because he knew that the warps were trailing out astern. He climbed in the wheelhouse and hauled the engine out of gear as it was still turning the propeller. By that time I was hanging over the side, I had been washed over too but I had got hold of a rope. There were ropes hanging over my shoulders. My father came to me and by this time I was way under the bilge of the boat. I had been under water but he managed to get me hauled up, so between me pulling and him hauling I got in on the deck. Then I got the water out of my stomach. I then went below to see conditions there, but by this time my brother had come on deck. So much water had gone down the hatch that the table in the cabin had been knocked up along the face of John William's bunk, so he could not get out and had had to push with his feet to shift the table away from his bunk. As he waded through water to get to the hatch, water was still pouring down.

"Anyway, the small boat was also adrift but the four men in the water managed to get to it and climb aboard. She was half full of water as there was no nile in her, but she had flotation tanks so she

Replenish after Vee Skerries. Photo: Clement J. Williamson

kept afloat. The oars had washed away but they got a piece of plank of some kind, whether it was floating or was it in the boat I could not say, and managed to paddle right up alongside and we got the four men out of the small boat. They were Harry Laurenson, his son Willie, James Robert Cumming, and my brother, Sam. They came alongside and we managed to get them aboard. We saw that the propeller was clear and no ropes hanging out over. Soon we got the ropes all cleared up and aboard then we had to get the boat pumped out. We then got the engine pump going and a hand pump on the deck as well. We got her pumped out so we could run the engine without affecting the gearbox with water. After we had got her dried out a good bit we got the propeller on her and we slowly came home. The wireless, aerials and everything were washed overboard so we had no means of communications with the other boats; by that time the boats would have been home anyway. We steamed slowly as she was listing heavily to port but we managed to come right up around and came in and anchored at Easter Dale.

"Obviously, nobody knew what had happened to us but some folk in Hamnavoe saw this strange looking boat heading for Easter Dale but did not recognise the *Replenish*. We managed to get her up to her moorings and came ashore with the small boat and headed for home. We got a lift part of the way in a van. Our wives and folk home wondered why we were dressed in very old clothes, old boiler suits and such like. Winnie, my wife, just stared at my clothes and only then did she hear what had happened to the boat. My father said we all had a lot to thank the Lord for that our lives were spared that day. It was a miracle that we all escaped with our lives.

"After a few weeks we got a temporary repair done at Scalloway, just enough to enable us to go to Fraserburgh and get a steel wheelhouse and galley to replace the smashed wooden one. After some weeks we travelled back to Fraserburgh and brought her home and fished with her until 1982 when she was sold. That was the story of our escapade at the Vee Skeeries in December 1957."

Stanley's wife Winnie now takes up the story.

"That morning when Stanley left the house it was between one and two o'clock. I looked out the window after he went and I thought I can go back to bed and sleep sound as it was a beautiful morning,

Stanley and Winnie. Courtesy Stella Ward

no wind and a little snow on the ground. Later on through the day, the wind had got up and it was now quite rough. The bairns were at school except for Joyce, a little one playing around the house, but I felt there was something wrong, as all the boats were coming back and no sign of the *Replenish*. Nothing from them on the radio, the other boats were speaking to one another, and I started to feel really worried. I phoned to Stanley's mother at 'Rockmount' and she said there was no need to worry as the boat would be gone to Walls for shelter. However, I was not to sure about that.

"Anyway the time passed and I kept looking out the windows but there was no sign of boat or men. Eventually I saw a van coming up towards the house, it stopped and Stanley got out carrying his kit bag. I thought, what is this he is wearing, it's not his sea clothes, so I went to meet him. I could now see a cut on his forehead and some blood and I asked if something had happened. Stanley said we would go in and get a cup of tea and then he would tell me what it was all about, and the story really shocked me. The main thing

Crew of Replenish, *1953.*

was they were all safe and well apart from some cuts and bruises. Three of them – Stanley, Willie Laurenson and Sam – had to go the Gilbert Bain Hospital for X-rays. There it was found that nothing was broken just bruises and cuts, and although feeling very shaken they all recovered, for which we were all thankful to the Lord, and that's my bit of the story."

THE ANONYMOUS LETTER

I REMEMBER hearing this story many years ago. An old woman called Mary had an evil tongue and never a good word to say about anyone. A much younger woman called Jean bore the brunt of Mary's slander, but always in an indirect way. What Mary had against Jean I do not know, and it was not part of the story.

In Scalloway at that time there were two mail deliveries every day, one in the morning and one in the afternoon. Folk could post a card on Monday night to tell a friend in the village that they would be visiting on Tuesday evening; that was how good the postal service was.

One morning Jean got a letter addressed in very shaky capital letters. There was nothing in the letter to say who it was from, and it was full of nasty insinuations and filth. Jean was disgusted, and she promptly put it in the fire without telling any of the family. However, a few days later over a cup of tea she confided to a close friend the contents of the letter, and they discussed who the sender might be. Mary's name was mentioned as a possibility and her friend advised her to go and see Scollay, the policeman. Jean would not do this, and anyway she had put the letter in the fire and so that was the end of it. However, it was not so as two weeks later she got another letter, addressed with the same shaky capital letters. This letter was the same, full of lies and obscenities, so Jean decided to take her friend's advice to visit the police station and see the officer in charge.

William Scollay was a very shrewd man. He listened to Jean's story and he examined the letter. "Shocking," he said. "Really shocking. Do you have any idea who might have sent this letter?"

"No, I just don't know," Jean replied. "The only person I can think of might be Mary, but I really could not say for sure. Mind you, she does not like me. She scowls at me and speaks ill of me to her neighbours."

Constable Scollay thought for a moment and then said, "I'll tell you what we will do. We will send the letter back to her."

PC William Scollay. Photo: Clement J. Williamson

Jean sat up, "Do you think that's a good idea? Maybe she will come to our door with it."

He smiled. "No Jean, I think not. She is too clever for that." He got a plain envelope and addressed it to Mary. Then he took the letter and on the back with a pencil put two marks in a corner. He showed the marks to Jean, put the letter in an envelope, stamped and sealed it. "I'll post it when it gets dark." he said.

"But supposing," said Jean, "it was not her that sent it."

"Then," replied the astute Constable William Scollay, "I will soon hear about it, as she has come here in the past with little tittle-tattle tales. We will just play a waiting game."

Two days later Jean made her way to the police station again. Constable Scollay smiled and said, "Well, Jean, come away in. Now what are you going to tell me this time?"

The Anonymous Letter

At Scalloway Police Station – PC Archie Nicolson and PC Donald Sutherland. Courtesy Arnold Duncan

Jean handed him an unopened envelope addressed to her with the same shaky capital letters as before. He opened it and took out the enclosed letter and looked at the back of the page, then held it out to Jean so she could see the two pencil marks. "Not very clever after all, is she? Well, we've got her fair and square this time. I'll guarantee you will not get any more letters from her."

In the afternoon the policeman visited Mary.

"My, my. Is dis you?" she said. "Come you away in and sit you down."

Once seated the constable asked, "Well, well, Mary, and how is your good self today?"

"Oh, I'm fine," replied Mary. "But I'm wondering why you're come to see me this day."

Constable Scollay looked at her severely and said, "Now, Mary, this filthy anonymous letters have got to stop, or I will take you over the hill to the Sheriff in Lerwick."

169

Mary jumped to her feet, bristled and raised her voice almost to a scream. She stamped her foot, and spat out, "Anonymous letters, how dare you come in here and accuse me of writing such a thing?"

The officer took the letter from his pocket and held it up for her to see, then turned it round so she could see the two pencil marks. "You see these pencil marks Mary? I put them there before I posted this letter to you. Yes Mary, I posted the letter to you and you sent it back to Jean. I know all about it. Any more letters and it will be six months at least in the cells for you."

Mary sat down and the officer continued, "How would you like that, eh?"

Police cell windows, Scalloway. Photo: Willie Smith

AROUND SCALLOWAY

SCALLOWAY, like many other places in Shetland, has changed much over the years, most significantly with either the closure of businesses or their passing into other hands. This is, of course, a naturally occurring process. However, since the last war and

Blacksness Pump.

the coming of oil development, people and premises have been replaced to such an extent and in so short a time that a visitor returning to scenes of earlier years would find the place changed beyond all recognition. Everything has not gone, but so much has been added and lost that it is worthwhile to look back to the first of the century.

Blacksness Stores.

Blacksness staff.

Around Scalloway

In the 19th century, in the spring of 1844, Hay & Co., Lerwick, commenced fish curing at Blacksness, and a shop was opened in June of that year for the sale of goods and strong drink. Scalloway was a base for spring cod fishing; smacks operated from there and also engaged in early herring fishing. A post office was opened in 1850 in Hay's shop, with Gilbert Tulloch as sub-postmaster. Hay & Co. also opened a second shop in Scalloway's Main Street in 1855, but this was closed in 1857.

Hay's shop at Blacksness, named Blacksness Stores, was soon well stocked with a great variety of materials including coal, salt, and building materials of all kinds. Men were employed all winter making barrels in the cooperage, and small boat building commenced in the north yard under foreman carpenter Malcolm Laurenson. He had as apprentices Thomas Walter Scott, Scalloway;

RAF slipway (post-war) and carpenter's workshop. Photo: Clement J. Williamson

Walter Duncan, Hamnavoe; Harry Laurenson, Skeld; and James Williamson, Scalloway. All these men in their day turned out first class Shetland model boats.

Telegraph communication was brought to the post office in 1870 and, as more space was required, Hay & Co. built a large new shop. Ogilvy Jamieson, who was Hay's shop manager, became the

Blacksness; post office on right. Photo: Clement J. Williamson

Blacksness shop. Photo: Clement J. Williamson

The end of the Blacksness shop. Photo: Clement J. Williamson

first agent for the north boats which had commenced running a west side service. Blacksness Pier was extended, and a new store for steamers' goods was built in 1896.

Hay & Co. had many employees and their hours of work were controlled by a bell, suspended in a small wooden belfry mounted on a shed opposite the shop door. The bell was rung to start work at 6am, then at 9am for breakfast, and at 10am to start again; at 2pm for dinner and 3pm to start, and lastly at 6pm when work finished. Long before the days of radio and hearing Big Ben, the folks in Scalloway set their clocks and watches by the sound of the Blacksness bell.

The post office was moved into Blacksness House, with David Williamson as postmaster. Alice Morrison and her daughter, Gladys Copland, took over in 1901 and between them held the post until 1962. Gladys' husband Basil worked in the office as well and as youngsters we thought he was the postmaster. Sixty-one years was a truly wonderful period of service by one family. The post office then relocated to Lovers Lane with Donnie Jamieson as postmaster. Sonny Bruce took over when Donnie and family moved to the south, and when Sonny retired, the post office was on the move again, relocating to the old butcher shop on Main Street with Maisie Reid

WILLIE'S TALES & TRAVELS

Celia gets her pension from Gladys at Blacksness Post Office. Photo: Clement J. Williamson

Long-serving Scalloway postman, Willie Scott. Photo: Clement J. Williamson

Around Scalloway

Donnie in Lovers Lane Post Office; Robbie Laurenson, Burnside, gets his pension. Photo: Clement J. Williamson

Sonny Bruce, Tootsie Thomson and Donnie Jamieson at Lovers Lane. Photo: Clement J. Williamson

177

Willie's Tales & Travels

as postmistress. On Maisie's sudden death, the post office was taken over by Mark and Helen Robinson. On their departure in 2007 to take over a shop in Weisdale, it was run for an interim period by Janice Morrison. In 2008, it was on the move again, west along Main Street to the premises vacated by George Johnson, Plumber and heating engineer, and now Yealtaland Bookshop. Owner of the bookshop, Dr Andrew Jennings, became the new postmaster with Janice Morrison as assistant.

Post Office, Main Street. Photo: Willie Smith

Phillip in Main Street Post Office. Photo: Willie Smith

AROUND SCALLOWAY

Andrew and staff Amanda, Janice and Carina at Post Office. Photo: Willie Smith

Many firms had fishcuring stations at Blacksness: Davidson and Gray; George Hughes; A. Flett, Buckie; and A. Davidson, Lerwick. In addition, John Harper of Wick had the north yard for curing, and G. Cormack, also of Wick, had the west side of the pier. Hay & Co.

Walter Duncan reports on fish landings. Photo: Clement J. Williamson

179

Willie's Tales & Travels

Selling fish from Pilot Us. *Photo: Clement J. Williamson*

Selling fish at Blacksness. Photo: Clement J. Williamson

Around Scalloway

Jim Duncan, Robert Smith and James Davidson from W. S. Uncles. Photo: Clement J. Williamson

Night landing. Photo: Clement J. Williamson

*John Robert Duncan, Alfie Jamieson and Walter
Duncan, auctioneer. Photo: Clement J. Williamson*

also cured white fish and used the stone-built kiln, which was later used by two brothers from Wick, Donald and William Wares. In my young days, the kiln and shed was W. S. Uncles of Glasgow with Willie Smith (not me) and James Davidson buying and shipping fish. In the 1960s some local men bought the premises, enlarged it, and it was called Iceatlantic. They processed fish and one of their products was boil-in-the-bag kipper fillets. Ships used to call at the pier and load frozen fillets etc. and sail to Boston, USA. Also working at the pier were two oil companies: the Anglo American Oil Co. Ltd

AROUND SCALLOWAY

Packing herring at east side, Blacksness. Photo: Clement J. Williamson

and the Scottish Oil Agency, supplying oil to the fishing boats as well as to the local shops for lamp oil. At that time there were seven shops in Scalloway selling paraffin, today there are none.

Oil and water being supplied to fishing boats. Photo: Clement J. Williamson

Tammie Henry, oilman. Photo: Clement J. Williamson

Around Scalloway

Between the wars, Laurence Mowat, who had acquired his grandfather's small smiddy (smithy) at New Street, built a larger smiddy at Blacksness. When Laurence retired the premises were taken over by the now defunct firm of Iceatlantic.

Laurence Mowat at anvil. Photo: Clement J. Williamson

WILLIE'S TALES & TRAVELS

The North of Scotland steamer called at Blacksness two or three times a week, and along the west side of Shetland with supplies for all the villages; and they had a hotel at Hillswick. I can remember when the new *St Clair* arrived in 1937. All the school children were marched along the High Road (Castle Street) to Blacksness and lined up along the pier, all waving flags and cheering. Then when the steamer had berthed we were all marched back to the school wondering what it was all about. At the outbreak of the Second World War, the *St Clair* was requisitioned by the government and that was the last of the steamers coming to Blacksness.

One time a union man arrived from Lerwick, held a meeting, and wanted the Scalloway dockers to go on strike. What it was about is lost in time. The steamer was going to be held up but one old docker knew that to go on strike would be no pay packet at the weekend. With a family to feed he could ill afford to go on strike so said, "I'll tell you what we will do boys, get the steamer loaded first, and then we will go on strike."

St Clair, *1930s. Photo: Clement J. Williamson*

AROUND SCALLOWAY

Getting ready for departure, 1930s. Photo: Clement J. Williamson

Steamer leaving Blacksness, 1930s. Photo: Clement J. Williamson

187

West side, Blacksness. Photo: Clement J. Williamson

    Leaving the Blacksness area, at the top of the brae on the left hand side was the joiner shop of Arthur Russell. Apprenticed to Russell were Mathew Sinclair, who later started a number of businesses in Sandwick, and William Hughson, who took over after Arthur Russell retired. Both kept up the high standard of workmanship that Russell demanded. I've heard a story about war meetings held in Hughson's workshop during World War One. In those days wireless sets were rare, if at all, and never much news filtered through to the general public. Newspapers only came at weekends, hence the war meetings. Men would gather of an evening in William Hughson's workshop to discuss what they thought was happening and what they thought would happen and should happen on the front. Young boys would gather in as well, to listen with excitement. One young boy, so the story goes, one night after stationing himself near the door, said he had a piece of poetry for them.

    He began:
"Between the anchor and the Somme,
There's many a one with thoughts of home."
There were murmurs of, "Ay ay, dat dey truly ir, poor boys."
The boy continued:
"Wondering what da aald folk will do,
When there's nobody hame tae torment dem noo."
Needless to say, he had to make a hurried exit.

Around Scalloway

Castle Camp Nissen hut. Photo: Clement J. Williamson

A.S.R. boat 2570. Courtesy Bob Garrett.

189

Seaplane in East Voe. Photo: Clement J. Williamson

I can remember as a boy looking through a crack in the door of the long disused workshop, and seeing William Johnson's concrete angel lying on a bench. In the wartime the angel was set in a castle window by some RAF boys (see Willie's War).

In the middle of Blacksness Brae were some small buildings in which folk lived. I can just remember them before the Brae was widened. At the top of the Brae was a little cottage; a man stayed in a room on the ground floor and above his room an old lady stayed. His chimney went on fire and a neighbour man set up a ladder and was going to pour water down the chimney. Whether by mistake or otherwise he poured the bucket of water down the old lady's chimney. Just imagine the scene. It defies description, fire blazing out the man's chimney and the old lady screeching about the water putting her fire out!

Much later the house was to have an addition at the front; the house was called Annslea. It was a tea room for a long time.

Further up the High Road, on the site of an old house, stands a house called Castle Garden. This old house was the home of the family of James Smith who had the first school in Scalloway. I can remember many years ago some elderly folk referring to Castle Garden as the Schoolhouse. There could not have been many pupils at the school as the building was not large.

Around Scalloway

Annslea, teas and waters. Photo: Clement J. Williamson

The old schoolhouse. Photo: Clement J. Williamson

WILLIE'S TALES & TRAVELS

At the peat stack in High Road quarry. Photo: Clement J. Williamson

After James Smith retired (he died in 1900), a number of doctors stayed there and a surgery was built. One doctor was Thomas Pretsell who constructed a small pier in the voe below the schoolhouse. It was called the Doctor's Pier, with enough water depth to take his cabin cruiser *Mimosa*, which was built at Westshore by Flaws and Johnson.

Beyond the east wall of the castle was a small stone-built shed where Jack Manson worked. Jack was deformed but did some light work, framing pictures and cutting out very fine name boards for fishing boats. He also was, I have heard, a gifted seascape painter, and perhaps some of his work can still be seen in the village today. I remember Gilbert Leask, a joiner, working in the shed in later years. Today, unfortunately, it is a ruin.

In the sixties or early seventies John Johnson had a men's haircutting shop, something lacking in Scalloway for some years.

At the south end of New Street stands a house named Da Noost, but formerly called Johnson's Buildings, after its builder, William Johnson from Wester Quarff. It was built as a tenement with a shop

Around Scalloway

Johnson's barber shop. Photo: Clement J. Williamson

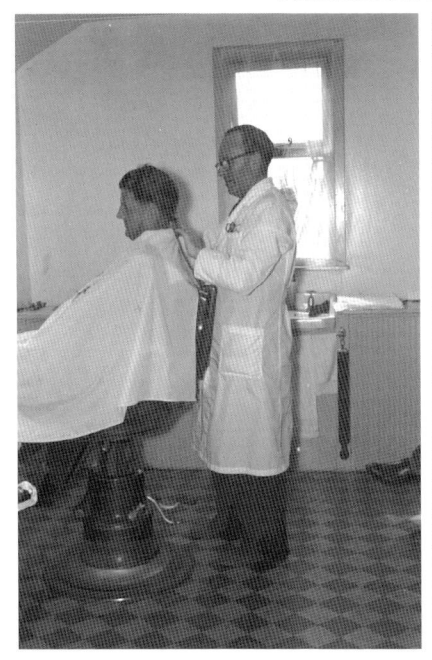

John Johnson trims Attie Williamson's hair. Photo: Clement J. Williamson

John Johnson's hairdressing shop and Blacksness sheds. Photo: Clement J. Williamson

Salvation Army on New Street. Photo: Clement J. Williamson

frontage on the street. No property in Scalloway has changed so often for business purposes. The following firms operated from the shop: John Moncrieff, shoemaker; Robert Fraser, draper; James Williamson, grocer; Mrs Duncan, grocer (later North Road, Lerwick); Laurence Flaws, grocer; C. Tulloch, restaurant; W. Johnson, grocer; Charleson Bros, grocers; Thomas Ogilvy, butcher (also of Lerwick); Scalloway Café and Restaurant; George Ross, confectioner; Kay Ross, knitwear; Robert Irvine, footwear; Yvonne, ladies' hairdresser; Pat Henry, ladies' hairdresser; J. Philips, ladies' and gents' hairdresser. In addition, at one time, a Miss Annie Colvin had a boarding house in the building with a notice that read, Miss Colvin's Comfortable Apartments, so I've heard.

While Laurence Flaws was the shopkeeper, he had a billiard table in a small back room. This raised the status of the place to the extent that the parish minister, the inspector of the poor and registrar, and the local doctor frequently met there for a game of a hundred up.

Around Scalloway

Johnnie delivers papers to Mary at 'Jeemie's'. Photo: Clement J. Williamson

Long load at Jeemsie's corner. Photo: Clement J. Williamson

Clement Williamson's father built a new shop and dwelling house on the corner of New Street, next door to Da Noost. However, the shop of James Williamson, merchant, who served in the shop with his son, Wilfie, was always called Jeemsie's. When I remember the shop first it had a wall back Tilley lamp, which gave off a good light. In the back shop, bacon was cut with a large knife and butter was weighed up on an old fashioned scale. As a young boy, I always liked to go in the shop as it had a homely atmosphere and there was always a friendly word from both Jeemsie and Wilfie. Quite often there was a sweetie as well. In the wartime, two of our four ration books were registered there. On the seaward side from the street they had a small garden with a greenhouse. The greenhouse had a large opening skylight and below it was an astronomical telescope. Wilfie and his brother, Clement, studied the stars and planets. I, too, would get the chance to look at the moon and planets and wonder how and why they all came into being.

Farther north along the street lived Captain James Tait, a retired seaman who had sailed many years as master with the Clyde Shipping Company, Glasgow. Just opposite his house he built a studio (now demolished) as his main hobby and pastime was photography. He took portraits in the studio, and also painted pictures. When Captain Tait died in 1927, Clement Williamson acquired The Studio and had it until his death in 1994. People came from all over Shetland to have their wedding photos taken by Clement.

Above: Clement and Thomasina Sinclair in The Studio door.
Right: Clement in The Studio.

Willie's Tales & Travels

Clement at The Studio door.

Brass Band, Studio Brae, 1917.

Around Scalloway

Next door to Captain Tait was a small house in which a Mary Inkster and her daughter did a small trade in dressmaking. The daughter was also at one time organist in the United Free Church, now The Kirk Business Centre.

The Scott family occupied the first house of New Street for many years, and for a time Walter Scott operated a small general merchant business. There was no piped water supply in those days, but in front of Walter Scott's shop was a well. I have an old hand written letter (courtesy of the late Jackie Thomson) that gives the locations of the many wells around Scalloway (see separate chapter). This one was at the top of the brae, about where the little concrete dyke joined the iron railings; it must have been a deep well as there was a pump on it. Walter was also a buyer of whelks, which he stored

Willie Isbister, pump at top of Studio Brae.

Willie's Tales & Travels

Tammie Burgess on Andrew Johnson's Clydesdales. Muckle Haa (or Scott's Haa) and Tarry Manse (also known of as Haa kitchens) on left. Photo: Clement J. Williamson

Demolition of Tarry Manse. Photo: Clement J. Williamson

in sacks in the sea at a small stone pier below his shop, waiting for shipment.

Muckle Haa doorway.

In the lower flat of the Muckle Haa, or Scott's Haa, there was another general merchant business, owned by Robert Turnbull, the son of Rev. John Turnbull, minister of Tingwall. A separate door, now blocked up, was used as the shop entrance. The rest of the Haa was occupied by different families.

Robert Turnbull, like some others of his family, met his death by drowning. A man by the name of Standen wanted to travel from Scalloway to Reawick on business and, as a sea route was much quicker than going by road, Robert Turnbull offered to transport him across in a small sailing boat he had just had built. A neighbour, Peter Sinclair, was in the boat with Robert Turnbull and Standen when they left Scalloway. Somewhere on the journey the boat capsized and Turnbull and Sinclair were both drowned, but Standen, who was a strong swimmer, survived. Jeemsie's father, William Williamson, was of the opinion that Turnbull's boat was over-rigged, carrying too much sail, and as such was unsafe. Whether the boat was found is not recorded.

Connecting New Street with Castle Street is a narrow lane called Smithy Lane (Smiddy Kloss) taking its name from the old smiddy which was in use many years ago; the ruins of it can still be seen half way up the lane. The last blacksmith who worked there was, I believe, a man called Scott Russell, reputedly a good tradesman.

Burn Beach; Mitchell Georgeson's house and workshop on right.

At the corner of New Road and New Street was the house of Mitchell Georgeson, Scalloway's best known master builder; a builder and architect whose fine work stands as a memorial among buildings in Scalloway today. His workshop was sited at the front of his house in New Road, but was long ago removed when the house was modernised. Among the fine buildings erected by Mitchell Georgeson were Scalloway Public Hall, Ingaville (for the Inkster family) and the Royal Hotel at West Shore (for James Reid). It is interesting to note that Mitchell Georgeson was the first builder in Scalloway to use concrete. This was a new experiment, and he used it to build his house at New Road. It speaks well for the workmanship that the house to this day stands without any cracking.

A well-known local personality and businessman later occupied the house. He was William Rae Duncan, one time manager of Hay & Co.'s business at Blacksness (more of him elsewhere). I have heard it said that the Royal Hotel was originally intended to be built at the corner of New Road and Main Street on part of what is now the Fraser Park. The ground belonged to the Garriocks of Gibblestone, and it seems no satisfactory agreement could be reached, so the hotel was built at West Shore where the Walter and Joan Gray Eventide Home stands today.

Ingaville, 1909.

Hughes Station at Garrick's. Photo: Clement J. Williamson

In one of the Bayview houses, MacNab of Perthshire, a firm of Scottish tweed manufacturers, employed two weavers to produce tweed, which was honestly marked 'Hand woven in the Shetland Isles'. Bob Little was the man in charge, and it was here that John Hunter, Scalloway's weaver poet, learned his trade.

The fine granite-built house on the corner of Main Street and now called Bona Vista was erected by W. Stevenson Smith, who used the ground floor as a shop, selling groceries and hosiery. The shop was managed by Alex F. Inkster, who later purchased the house and business, which he carried on until his retirement. Others who at one time ran a business in the property were Shetland Knitwear, J. Tait, J. Leask, Norman Gilbertson and Scalloway Museum.

The ground floor of the building next to Bona Vista was for many years occupied by Basil S. Copland, watchmaker and photographer. His studio was built on the corner of New Road. Basil S. Copland learned his trade with David Sutherland of Uyeasound, who had a watch repairing business in Lerwick. Many of Copland's photographs of local people and views are still to be found in old family albums in Scalloway. After Copland, John Smith of Berry Farm had a butcher shop, with Andy Thomson in charge. Norman Gilbertson took over the shop after Andy retired, and when Norman

Andy Thomson. Photo: Clement J. Williamson

moved to pastures new the butcher shop continued with the Watt brothers, Neil and Brian. When John Johnson's woollen factory became vacant, Neil and Brian acquired the premises and the little butcher shop became the post office, with Maisie Reid as postmistress. After Maisie came Mark and Helen Robinson then Andrew Jennings with Janice Morrison. The premises was latterly Hunter's Fish Shop but now stands empty. The first floor was the district council office, with Walter Mowat Sen. as clerk. Walter was also the registrar for the Tingwall area.

Quite a section of Scalloway's Main Street was occupied by a bakery business first started by a man called Laurence Moncrieff.

Hunter's Fish Shop. Photo: Willie Smith

Hunter's Fish Shop: Joan serves a customer. Photo: Willie Smith

Around Scalloway

It was later carried on by William Anderson. Then by Mowat & Co. who built up a large business supplying all kinds of bread and fancy cakes. I particularly remember their morning rolls, mince pies and baker's biscuits. We thought they were excellent and hard to beat. There are always changes and the premises are now part flats and a creche.

Mowat's bakers: Mac, Rasmie, Jock, Attie, Kelly. Photo: Clement J. Williamson

William Anderson.

Rasmie with bread made for Methodist Church harvest service. Photo: Clement J. Williamson

Congregational Church. Photo: Clement J. Williamson

Baptism in Congregational Church. Photo: Clement J. Williamson

Around Scalloway

Garriock & Co., fish merchants and owners of fishing smacks, had offices nearby, and in the same building the Union Bank of Scotland had an office. Next along the street was a house occupied by the Rev. Nicol Nicolson, minister of Scalloway Congregational Church. The Union Bank stood next to the minister's house, and Rev. Nicolson used to make a joke by saying that he and Mr Anderson were the two best off men in Scalloway, for they had a bank between them.

A building which was demolished to make way for the Fraser Park entrance was the office of Robert Inkster of Ingaville. He managed the affairs of a number of local fishing boats, as well as being a shareholder in many of them. When Inkster retired, Ross and Budge took over the premises for a joinery and funeral undertaking business. At that time there were three funeral undertakers in Scalloway!

Along the south side of Main Street, the old fish drying shed used by Garriock & Co. was taken over by H. Williamson & Sons, who ran a motor and radio repair business, and also had a petrol pump. It

Williamson's petrol pumps. Photo: Clement J. Williamson

was here that through their enterprise the east side of Scalloway got electric light, when they installed a 100-volt DC generator. At the other end of Scalloway, William Moore & Sons installed a 110-volt DC electric supply, so all of Scalloway had electric light. When eventually streetlights were erected, in the mid-1930s, a switching on ceremony was held in the public hall. Jack Moore and Jamie Williamson thought out a system to switch on, at the same time, two different supplies to two different sets of streetlights, one supply being 100 volts and the other 110 volts. Mr Moore Senior was reputed to have said they would blow the flaming place sky high when they pulled the switch. However, everything went very smoothly and Scalloway has had street lighting, ever since.

To the south of Garriock's fish drying shed was their kippering kiln. Other curers used the premises over the years, including the National Fishcuring Company who were the owners when, in 1963, a disastrous fire swept through the kiln and burned it to the ground.

National fishworkers. Photo: Clement J. Williamson

AROUND SCALLOWAY

National Kiln well alight. Photo: Clement J. Williamson

The building opposite the bank housed tenants on the upper floor, while the ground floor was a large and well stocked store owned by Robert Fraser who, with his brother Francis Fraser, gifted the Fraser Park to Scalloway. Fraser's shop sold groceries, drapery, hardware, newspapers, meat and dairy produce. A dressmaking and millinery business was conducted on the upper floor, while John Moncrieff had part of the ground floor for shoe repairs, where he employed two or three hands. At this time in Scalloway there were six or seven different shops where boots and shoes could be repaired. Today there are none.

Two bonny National lasses. Photo: Clement J. Williamson

WILLIE'S TALES & TRAVELS

Robert Fraser. Courtesy Neil Watt.

Fraser workers. Courtesy Neil Watt.

Adam Jamieson in doorway. Courtesy Neil Watt.

With the departure of Robert Fraser to Aberdeen, Adam Jamieson, an enterprising member of his staff, acquired the grocery and butcher's business. He gave much attention to his activities and the shop bore the sign, Jamieson. Adam, as he was popularly known, was a member of the Congregational Church and served on many public committees. At the end of World War One he was awarded the MBE.

After Adam's death the business was run for a time by Nicolson & Co., and finally by Walter Duncan who had served in the shop so faithfully since first being employed by Adam Jamieson. After World War Two the building was bought by John Johnson for use as a woollen factory. The small shop was a dairy for a time and then a fancy goods shop run by J. Leask. Today, Scalloway Meat Company occupies the whole building with the ground floor selling all kinds of groceries, confectionery, bread (with in-store bakery), newspapers and magazines, beers, wines and spirits and a very well stocked and popular butcher department. On the first floor you can find all kinds of household goods, clothing and footwear, toys and

WILLIE'S TALES & TRAVELS

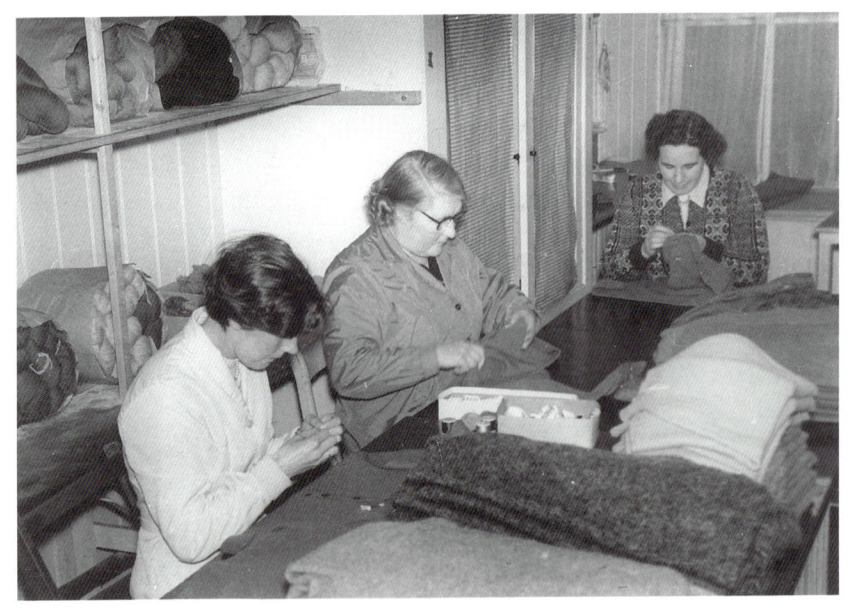

Woollen Company workers, c.1970s. Photo: Clement J. Williamson

Scalloway Meat Co. 2011. Inset: Butcher Danny Christie. Photos: Willie Smith

AROUND SCALLOWAY

fancy goods and all kinds of greetings cards. Neil Watt is the very able sole proprietor.

Beyond the Gibblestone garden, and on a site now taken over by the Scalloway Hotel, stood a little sweetie shop owned by Bobby Nicolson, known locally as Minna's (see Willie's War).

Donald McInnes, then head teacher at Scalloway new school, built the Scalloway Hotel with Mrs McInnes as proprietor of this new enterprise. Following McInnes, the hotel was taken over by Charles Lennie and it was during his ownership that a disastrous

Scalloway Hotel. Photo: Clement J. Williamson

Scalloway Hotel 2011. Photo: Willie Smith

fire entirely gutted the building. It was, however, rebuilt in a very short time. Since then the hotel has changed ownership a number of times, later owners being Pat Castle, J. Forsythe, James Halcrow, William Burnett, George Spence, who modernised and enlarged it greatly, Norman Gilbertson, Abdul Zaoui, Sam and Dot Davis, and the present owners are Peter and Caroline McKenzie who have upgraded and modernised the business. What was then the bar of the hotel opened off the Lang Closs, and I remember it as the Hygenic Stores, George Ross's shop, selling groceries, which closed just after the war.

Across the lane, now called Gibblestone Road, but formerly the Lang Kloss, was the grocer's shop owned by G. Kay of Lerwick, which was closed before World War One. The next occupants were R. and C. Nicolson, chemists. Walter Williamson took over after the Nicolsons and, on Walter's death, the business was carried on by Mrs Jeanette Williamson. When she retired it became Lyons, grocers, and later the premises of George H. Johnson, Plumber and Heating Engineer. It is now Yealtaland Books and Post Office.

Further up the Lang Kloss was a cooperage where I remember Willie Manson at work making barrels. There was also a slaughterhouse in the yard, run by Andy Thomson the butcher.

The Gospel Meeting Hall was built as a bakehouse by William Anderson Thomson in 1930, and closed about the time of the outbreak of the war. It was later used for making concrete blocks by T. Smith & Son with Willie Burnett and Walter Halcrow Senior. David Fotheringham then had the building for a joinery workshop. James Johnson & Sons had a haulage business, initially using horses, which soon gave way to motorcars and lorries. This firm ran a bus service between Lerwick and Scalloway very successfully, and as business increased they moved to larger premises at Garriock's yard. The firm was finally taken over by Sutherland Transport for haulage only and has now ceased.

Lantern show in hall, early 1930s.

Adjacent to the public hall was the firm of building contractors, Charles Abernethy. Upon Abernethy leaving for Australia, George Nicolson and James Coutts continued the business. Part of Abernethy's former workshop was taken over by Alexander Cromarty, who ran a motor hiring business and bus service to Lerwick. Leaving Scalloway, Cromarty sold out to Georgeson and Moore, who in their turn sold out to Andrew Morrison and Alan Young who renamed the firm Shalder Coaches. In the 1990s, P&O Ferries began running a weekly trip to Bergen with the St Clair, and Andrew Morrison organised bus tours to Norway and Sweden. They were very popular. Rapsons of Inverness acquired Shalder Coaches but they since closed and sadly Scalloway, which had two bus companies since buses started running, now has no bus company.

In a large two-storey building, now demolished, and on the site of the present Royal Bank of Scotland, was the Commercial Bank of Scotland Ltd., and also the parish council office and the office of the registrar. This post was held by David Beaton, and before him his father, Charles Beaton, so the building was called Beaton's House.

Behind Beaton's House were two buildings, called (for obvious reasons) Da Widden Hoose and Da Stein Hoose, one wood and the other of stone. These were built for workers by Smiths of Aberdeen and rightly called Smith's Buildings. Each tenant had two rooms without running water, and an outside toilet. Da Widden Hoose was demolished in 1947 and the wood sold. The main joists were pitch pine, and the whole building was lined with V-lining. The wood was soon snapped up by local folk for sheds and gates and lining new extensions. Da Stein Hoose still stands today, as do its coal sheds, Da Tin Sheds.

'Da Widden Hoose' 1900s.

Crew at Christie's about 1910.

Herring curing and kippering took place where the Kiln Bar and Restaurant now stands. Some of the firms in this line of business were A. Christie, D. Wares, Dan Harper, D. MacKenzie and R. Burgess. Part of the kiln was badly damaged by fire in the 1930s. The arrival of fire fighting apparatus from Lerwick saved the main part of the building.

Christie at Red Kiln.

WILLIE'S TALES & TRAVELS

Red Kiln, 1915.

Harcus Linklater, Beaton's House, R.&C. Nicolson, 1970. Photo: Clement J. Williamson

Around Scalloway

The large draper shop of Harcus, Linklater & Co. stood on the corner of Main Street and Chapel Lane (Harcus Kloss in my young days). The Harcus family who founded this business were, I believe, from Orkney. The business was very well stocked and staffed. It also had a tailoring service, in which worked Robert Thomson, his son Bob, and daughter Isa. The firm also traded in whelks. A wooden pier seaward from the shop was known as Harcus Pier, where the whelks were stored in bags in the sea while waiting shipment to markets in the south. The shop premises has changed owners and names a few times in recent years but is now a well-stocked grocer shop called The Checkout.

Checkout 2011. Photo: Willie Smith

Opposite Harcus' shop, and at the foot of Chapel Lane, was a butcher shop owned by James Nicolson of Utnabrake and managed by Erasmus Thomson, a prominent member of the Scalloway Methodist Church. He was later forced to retire, as failing eyesight unfortunately resulted in total blindness. Rasmie, as he was known locally, stayed at Ladysmith, and as an old man used to be taken out for walks and exercise by Ian Watt. I and other young boys got to know that if we said loudly, "Hello Rasmie," he would ask Ian who it was, and then dip his hand in his pocket and give us a penny.

Sunday morning, Methodist Chapel. Photo: Willie Smith

Methodist Church 1950s. Photo: Willie Smith

AROUND SCALLOWAY

Drama in Methodist Church, 1950s. Photo: Willie Smith

Methodist Church 1950s. Photo: Willie Smith

Following Rasmie in the shop as butcher was a Canadian called Garnet Atkinson, who lodged in our house at Hillside Road (then called Da Wast Back Road). He later was an insurance collector in Lerwick. James and George Morrison purchased the shop premises at the war's end, and George ran it as a grocer shop. They

Garnet Atkinson. Photo: Clement J. Williamson

previously had a shop in what had been the bar at the Royal Hotel. It was known locally as Dodie's. The new shop was also known as Dodie's and after George retired it became a ladies' hairdresser, run by Yvonne Sinclair, and is now a dwelling house.

A fairly large house on Main Street, called McGuires, opposite Dodie's, was at one time used as a bakery by Charles and William Reid, and later as a grocer shop by Laurence Flaws, who at that time had another grocer shop on New Street. It later became a dwelling house.

Immediately behind Nicolson's butcher shop, and on the present site of Da Galley Shed, stood the house of Dr Robertson. He was one of the old style doctors who practised without a licence from any authority. When examinations were introduced for would-be doctors, some of the older practitioners who had put in many years in the profession were given an exemption from examination. One such was Dr Robertson who, without modern medical knowledge, seemed to have had quite remarkable success in the profession. Dr Robertson had four daughters, and a son called Thomas who had the local nickname of Tammie Rittie. Clement said he remembered Thomas as a white-haired, white-moustached, rather taciturn man. He had a small shop in the same building, selling such things as ointments, plasters, corn cures, etc. which did not require a chemist on the premises. When spoken to, according to Clement, he would blow and snort through his nose, and often nobody understood whether this meant yes or no.

Some years later, this shop of Robertson's was acquired by Harry Williamson from Brae, who did quite a business in cycles, radio and motor repairs, before moving to more spacious premises in Main Street. Basil Copland, watchmaker, acquired this shop after Williamson, and finally it was pulled down and a new building erected for Mowat's Minerals. I can remember as a very young boy being in Basil's shop with my father and being fascinated by the shelves of clocks, all ticking away. The building is now the Galley Shed.

A small shop on the seaward side of the road was for many years run by Nellie Christie. She sold confectionery, ice cream and tobacco. Young men would gather there of an evening to banter and

225

discuss the events of the day. Later, George Ross had the shop, and in the first part of World War Two young soldiers and Norwegians would call along during the day to stand around and chat (see Willie's War). Georgeson and Moore had the shop for an office after the war, but it is now gone.

Fish and chip shop and Tammie Thomson's haircutting shop in front of Methodist Church. Photo: Clement J. Williamson

Chip shop fire. Photo: Clement J. Williamson

Around Scalloway

In Chapel Lane (Harcus Kloss) there was a small business called The Sheiling, owned by a Mrs E. Thomson who traded in Shetland knitted goods, while further up the lane Tammie Thomson doubled as a shoe repairer and hairdresser. On the site of where the Methodist Hall now stands was a fish and chip shop, built and owned by Andrew Robertson, who was followed on by John Walterson, and after him Harry Cook. John had the talent to be able to draw a caricature of anyone you asked him to. At one time I had drawings of weel kent local faces, now sadly lost.

West along the street we come to the house called Dinapore, built by Dr De Silva in the first part of the last century and named after his hometown in India. Dr De Silva had been an assistant to Dr Robertson of Lerwick before coming to practice in Scalloway. A native of India, he was a really good-natured man and well liked by all his patients. Dr James Smith acquired the house and surgery sometime during World War One. Dr Smith installed a small X-ray plant in the premises and it was put to good use. This may well have been the first X-ray plant in Shetland. Dr James Henderson Yule moved to the house in 1917. He was the son of Dr Mortimer Yule of Lerwick, a number of whose descendants have successfully pursued careers in the medical profession.

Dinapore. Photo: Willie Smith

WILLIE'S TALES & TRAVELS

Further west we come to the Walter and Joan Gray Eventide Home, a building which was originally the Royal Hotel, built for James Reid by Mitchell Georgeson Builder. There was a succession of owners before the building was bought and gifted to the Church of Scotland by Walter Gray, for an eventide home. Walter Gray was a Scalloway man whose successful career with the Marconi wireless company had seen him appointed assistant manager of that company in Canada. Part of the agreement was that he would have a room in the home, and he was a well-known figure in the village for some years.

Above: Royal Hotel. Left: Walter Gray.
Photos: Clement J. Williamson

Around Scalloway

Next door to the home was a small shop and a two-roomed cottage, the property of T. M. Adie & Sons. The shop was once occupied, I've heard, by a man called Magnus whose surname has been lost with the passage of time. He sold general goods, and had both milk and buttermilk in large jars on his counter. There is a story that one morning a large black cat leapt into the buttermilk jar. Once it had been rescued the buttermilk had to be poured away and the jar washed and cleaned, so there was no more buttermilk that day. Some neighbours, hearing of Magnus' predicament, and by way of a joke, sent their children to his shop with jugs or pails for a penny worth of buttermilk. Magnus was almost in tears, and saying, "Oh, what a buttermilk I could have sold today if it had not been for that blasted cat."

After Magnus, John Laurenson, a shoe repairer and hairdresser (I can remember having my hair cut by Uncle John, as we called him, by the light of a wall back oil lamp) had the shop for many years before it passed to Willie Blance, a gents' hairdresser.

John Laurenson (right) and James Davidson (centre) with unknown (left).

Sunday afternoon at the corner of John Laurenson's shop.

Following Willie's death, after World War Two Jemima Smith (Mimie) opened a tearoom, called the West Shore Tea Room, and built a small extension at the back. When the cottage became vacant it was joined to the café to make a larger dining area. After Mimie

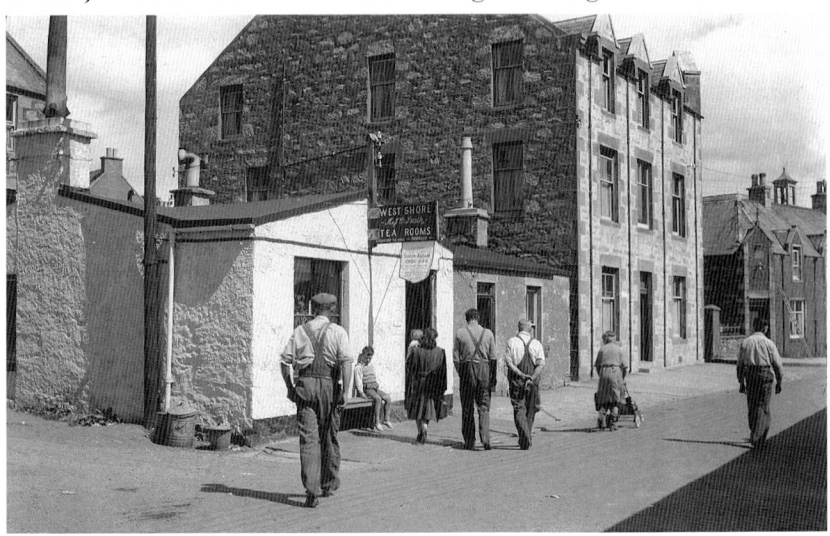

Howarth's men go to lunch. Photo: Clement J. Williamson

Around Scalloway

Da Ben End. Photo: Willie Smith

retired, I bought the premises for a joiner's workshop and DIY shop. When I stopped using the workshop end of the building my wife, Vera, and my sister, Anna, opened a tearoom called Da Ben End. Some years later failing health, unfortunately, forced its closure.

The Church of Scotland were about to demolish the Walter and Joan Gray Eventide Home (the ex Royal Hotel) and erect a new home and day care centre on

Da Ben End fireplace. Photo: Willie Smith

231

WILLIE'S TALES & TRAVELS

Church of Scotland. Photo: Clement J. Williamson

Anna, Joey and Vera in Da Ben End. Photo: Willie Smith

Around Scalloway

Da Ben End. Photo: Willie Smith

Rev. Harold and Maisie Bowes lend a hand. Photo: Willie Smith

Nell, Vera and Anna in Da Ben End. Photo: Willie Smith

the site. I sold them the old shop and cottage building, which they demolished too, rebuilding it as the day care centre.

From the shop end, a road leads up towards Adie's House, now modernised into self-contained flats, and on to what were the premises of Andrew Johnson. He owned two Clydesdale horses with carts and gigs, and a dairy. The dairy cattle were kept all day in the East Park, below the school. They were driven through the village at milking time, kept at the dairy overnight, and driven back to the park in the morning. The coming of motors did away with the horses and carts, but the firm of Andrew Johnson moved forward to hiring cars and lorries.

Adie's Station, built to seaward, was the scene of much activity during the herring season, with boats landing their catches at the long wooden pier. A firm with the name of Jenkins had a curing yard there for many years. There was no public hall at that time so many dances and functions were held in the commodious upper floor of Adie's store. A small club, called the Daisy Club, met there and boasted a fife and drum band which no doubt inspired Thomas Arthur, a baker and poet, to write the lines:

Oh who would be a Daisy,
And with the Daisies stand.
Upon the floor of Adies store,
Among the happy band.

During the war years the upper part of the store was first used by the NAAFI for a canteen. When going past there you could feel the smell of beer, and if we had money we would get soldiers to buy us chocolate, which by this time was rationed. Later, when camps were built in the village, they all had their own NAAFI canteens and the Norwegians used part of the store in connection with the Shetland Bus operations.

Uncle Robbie had a section for a workshop, which was used by the firm of Thomas Smith & Son, building contractors, who acquired the whole building at a later date. During the wartime, the ground floor was partitioned to make two dining rooms, one side for the regular soldiers and the other for the Home Defence. Outside, a cookhouse was built to serve both (see Willie's War). When the war finished, David Howarth used the ground floor for a carpenter's shop and had the large yard for building boats. Later still, the building became a youth centre, but at this moment it is empty.

Ladysmith and Howarth's yard. Adie's store on right. Photo: Clement J. Williamson

WILLIE'S TALES & TRAVELS

A three-storey building further west along the Main Street, built as a hotel, was managed at one time by Donald McInnes and his wife. When the new Scalloway school was built in 1876, Donald McInnes was appointed first headmaster and Mrs McInnes continued to run the hotel. The school was extended in 1910. At some time the hotel was taken over by Mr James Reid for a while before he had the new Royal Hotel built, and the building is now a dwelling house. Across the road was the weaving shed of T. M. Adie & Sons, Voe. A number of people were employed at hand weaving looms, turning out tweed.

One such worker I remember was John James Hunter, who got the name the Weaver Poet. He wrote a lot of poems and had two books published, Trums an Truss and Taen wi da Trow. Born in Scalloway in 1871, and dying in 1948, he stayed in a little cottage, now derelict, at the top of Hillside Road (Da Wast Back Road) with his wife, Georgina. They kept hens and ducks at the top of the hill above Ladysmith in an upturned boat called "Da Horse House". Trums an Truss proved very popular and rapidly sold out. The proceeds from the sale of the book went to the Church of Scotland.

John and Georgina Hunter. Photo: Clement J. Williamson

AROUND SCALLOWAY

The weaver poet. Photo: Clement J. Williamson

At the horse house. Photo: Clement J. Williamson

Willie's Tales & Travels

I don't know much about the history of the Weaving Shed, except that it had been connected with the herring station. The big door on the street was where they used to tip salt to the ground floor to be stored. People stayed in all the upper rooms, probably some were workers for the station. In the wartime the ground floor became the slipway engine room and carpenter's shop for the Shetland Bus operation.

At the junction of Main Street and Hillside Road stands a building which formerly housed the long established business of Nicolson & Company, founded by Charles Nicolson. This modern shop was built in 1906. Later the business was taken over by Charles's son, Gideon Nicolson, and David Dalgliesh, as partners. They in turn passed on the business to their sons, Charles David Nicolson and Laurence Sinclair Dalgliesh. During their period of ownership, a small branch shop was opened in Meadowfield Road, where many new houses were being built. This shop, under the name of Nicolson and Dalgliesh, was until quite recently run by Margaret Dalgliesh, daughter of L. S. Dalgliesh. It is now Springbank Electronics and run by Tom Deyell. The West Shore business passed into the hands of George Ross at the end of the war, still retaining the name of Nicolson & Company. Later it was bought by the partnership of John Smith and George Jamieson, who opened a branch shop at Berry Road, with Lyla Smith serving behind the counter. To all customers the shop then became known as Lyla's. Sadly, all that is in the past, and the once busy modern West Shore shop has been converted into flats. Lyla's is now the very popular Scalloway Charity Shop.

Across the road from Nicolson & Co. was a building which stood end-on to the street. In the gable there was a large show window and a door leading on to the first floor. In here was a shop dealing in ladies' outfitting, owned and run by Miss A. J. Nicolson. This shop was very modern for the time, as its owner planned its style and appearance; and it was, I understand, very well patronised by people of the district.

On the marriage of Miss Nicolson to Laurence Sinclair Dalgliesh, the shop was closed. Miss Nicolson's brother, Robert Nicolson, who had qualified as a dentist in Glasgow started a dental surgery there. I can remember as a seven-year-old having a tooth pulled out there

Around Scalloway

Nicolson & Co. with John Smith and a salesman in the doorway. Photo: Clement J. Williamson

and I was very noisy, I believe. Bobby, as he was known, said he always felt the pain more than the patient. He turned the large show window into an aviary, and kept canaries and budgies inside. It was very interesting for all and was called Da Birdie Window. Alas it is no longer there, part of the building having been removed for road widening. Beneath the shop my father had the joiner business of Thomas Smith & Son. The rest of the building comprised rented accommodation.

William Moore, an Orcadian, moved to Scalloway with his family after arriving back from the United States, and worked as a blacksmith in sheds across from the joiner shop. The venture was very successful, and with the motorisation of fishing boats the firm of William Moore & Sons grew into a vastly extended business with a marine engineering workshop, two slipways and a carpenter shop. Today the business is known as Malakoff and Moore, and with the downturn in the fishing industry the once busy engineering shop looks empty and neglected. The new slipway still has boats, but they are mainly from the salmon industry.

Da Birdie Window. Photo: Willie Smith

As a ten-year-old, I went and asked Mr Moore to sharpen a three-quarter-inch wood chisel for me. When he had done so, he said, "Now boy, before you start to use it, count all your fingers and thumbs."

It was in the mid-thirties that William Moore & Sons, together with H. Williamson & Sons, joined in a scheme to supply Scalloway with electric light. Moores had a single cylinder engine driving the dynamo, and the thump-thump it made was a comforting sound to a young boy after going to bed at night in the wartime.

James Andrew Thomson, who was born in Scalloway in 1902, and died in 1987, lived in Springbank, Houl Road (Da Back Road). In the mid-1950s he built a smiddy workshop in Da Watery Quarry, half-way up Hillside Road (Da Wast Back Road). Jeemsie, as he was known locally, worked with William Moore & Sons as a marine engineer and blacksmith, but what gave him the greatest pleasure was making ornamental iron craftwork. Jeemsie was a master craftsman and everything was made to perfection. His work was in great demand with locals and tourists alike. A craft shop in London sold a lot of his work, and he could turn out any ironwork on request.

Jeemsie. Photo: Clement J. Williamson

Beating out a paper-knife. Photo: Clement J. Williamson

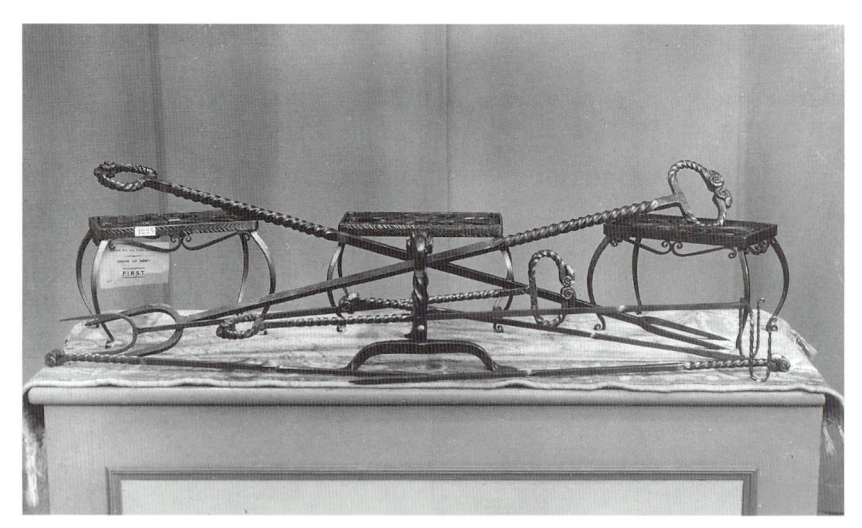

WILLIE'S TALES & TRAVELS

Display of Jeemsie's work. Photo: Clement J. Williamson

Jeemsie at forge. Photo: Willie Smith

In the 1920s, a two-storey building to be used for the repair of nets, was built by my father and Uncle Robbie for the firm of Nicolson & Co. at the foot of Ladysmith Road, on the site of a kippering kiln once owned by R. Christie. (Two years ago, while recladding the building, William Mouatt found the name R. Smith, my uncle.) Quite a number of local women were employed there mending nets. On the ground immediately behind, another building was planned, for the purpose of weaving nets. Although a start was made and concrete foundations laid, the work was halted and nothing more came of the project. The Netloft, as it was called, was requisitioned by the military at the outbreak of World War Two, and was used to billet troops for a time. With the arrival of Norwegians and the Shetland Bus operations (see Willie's War) it became a billet and cookhouse for the Norwegians, and the locals called it Norway House, a name still used today.

In Ladysmith Road, a kippering and curing business was started by an Aberdeen firm called J. M. Davidson. The firm was taken over by Lowrie Williamson in 1922 and continued with the Williamson family until 1987, when their operations were moved to more modern premises in Lerwick. Hjaltland Housing Association built modern flats on the site of the old kiln and the development is rightly called Lowries. Ladysmith was the name given to a row of houses built on the hillside above the kiln at the time of the siege of Ladysmith in the Boer War of 1900.

At the easternmost end of Port Arthur Road, in a large stone-walled garden full of old trees, stands a house built by one of the Garriocks of Berry. Next to it is the remains of a house said to belong to Sir Andrew Mitchell of Westshore. In this house, John Flaws and Laurence Johnson had a carpentry and boat-building business before World War One. It was from their yard that the *Mimosa*, a carvel built cabin cruiser, was built for Dr Thomas Pretsell. It is said that the boat was later sold to the Admiralty and used at Swarbacks Minn during the war.

A small wooden shed at the side of the Port Arthur road served as a workshop for George Watt, a shoe repairer. In one of the windows stood some stuffed birds, and as children we used to hurry past the shed, as the birds were rather fierce looking.

WILLIE'S TALES & TRAVELS

West Shore with Garriock's house and Sir Andrew Mitchell's house.

Yoal at West Shore.

Around Scalloway

West Shore (Nicolson's area) before Nicolson's shop.

Old houses, West Shore and George Watt's shed. Photo: Clement J. Williamson

WILLIE'S TALES & TRAVELS

Hillside, West Shore, 1940s. Photo: Clement J. Williamson

Hillside, West Shore, 2009.

Port Arthur, and the many herring curing stations sited there, were constructed by a Wick curer, Sandy Ronaldson, during the period of the Russo-Japanese war. At that time the seaport of Port Arthur featured much in the news from the east, hence the name. The construction of Port Arthur was a tremendous undertaking as, there being no roadway, the hillside had to be dug down to make a piece of level ground for stations and a road. The seafront had to be built rather loosely by stones.

Britannia, *LK140*, *ashore at Port Arthur road. Photo: Willie Smith*

Terraces were cut from the side of the west hill to site wooden huts for the women workers, and water was piped down from the hill. A concrete kiln was also built, and used by Dan Harper, also a Wick curer. During his occupancy a fire destroyed the roof. This was replaced but the building was never again used as a kiln. After Ronaldson gave up at Port Arthur, Tom Brown, a Lerwick curer, repaired the roadway, which had fallen into great disrepair, and resumed curing herring for a few years. Tom Brown was followed for a short time by a J. Slater.

WILLIE'S TALES & TRAVELS

It was during all this clearing and digging, all done by hand pick and shovel, that the curious old hillside hole called Robbie Rolly was destroyed as a local landmark. People wondered why it was so called, and the probable answer was given to Clement Williamson on a visit to Maggie Ann Watt on her 91st birthday. Maggie Ann was organist in the Scalloway Methodist Chapel for many years, and on this visit to her house she played and sang for Clement. The

Sunday afternoon at Rolly's, 1940s. Back: John Thomson, Willie Smith, Jackie Williamson. Front: Willie Fullerton, Ninkie Watt, Peter Laurenson, Jim Smith, Andy Smith.

explanation she gave was that a preacher who came to Scalloway sometime in the past had no church or place to hold meetings, so he held them in the open air at the hole in the hillside. The name of the preacher was Robert Roland, so it is easy to see how the name Robbie Rolly was given to the meeting place.

Robbie Rolly, from a painting by James Tait.

During World War Two, the Royal Artillery had a gun battery at Port Arthur. After the war, the Zetland County Council took over the dilapidated road and provided a retaining wall and fence, making access to Port Arthur much better.

Lowrie Williamson took over the old kiln and had a curing station there for some years. The old kiln had a roof, but no windows or doors. As an apprentice joiner, I was given the job to make the windows, under the direction of George Nicolson. For a number of years Lowrie had a second-hand furniture store there, with Davie Umphray doing repairs and restoring pieces of furniture. After Lowrie Williamson finished with curing herrings, Bobby Walterson bought the old kiln for a workshop. He constructed a slipway to the kiln so that the local lifeboats could be hauled up and taken inside for their annual overhaul. The old kiln is now gone, and on its site stands the North Atlantic Fisheries College. Many houses adorn the hillside at Port Arthur now, and continue on as far as the Red Geo. Scalloway has grown over the years and is still growing.

WILLIE'S TALES & TRAVELS

Port Arthur Road. Photo: Clement J. Williamson

Port Arthur kiln. Photo: Clement J. Williamson

Around Scalloway

Splitting herring at 'Lowrie's': Dovie, Aggie, Bertha, Celia, Teenie and Nellie. Photo: Clement J. Williamson

Scord Quarry 1930s. Photo: Clement J. Williamson

Willie's Tales & Travels

Scalloway Golf Club, 1920s-1930s. Photo: Clement J. Williamson

The first Scalloway school football team. From left -back: Sonny Copland, Willie Burgess, James Slater, Phillip Ward, Davie Slater, Attie Williamson. Front: John Smith, Gerald Watt, Bertie Burgess, Willie Young, Jim Wishart. Taken in Ingaville garden. Photo: Clement J. Williamson

Around Scalloway

A smoke and tea in the peat hill. Photo: Clement J. Williamson

Bairns used to swim at Bool Green. Photo: Clement J. Williamson

Willie's Tales & Travels

Having fun in the paddling pool. Photo: Clement J. Williamson

Opening of swimming pool. Photo: Clement J. Williamson

AROUND SCALLOWAY

Milk supply, 1947. Photo: Clement J. Williamson

Milk supply, 1955. Photo: Willie Smith

WILLIE'S TALES & TRAVELS

Billy and Billy 1955. Photo: Willie Smith

Mill Brae, 1955. Photo: Willie Smith

Around Scalloway

The Norseman, *Bob Yonson at bow, late 1940s. Photo: Willie Smith*

257

WELLS AROUND SCALLOWAY

A FEW YEARS AGO, the late Jackie Thomson gave me some information about wells in Scalloway written by an unknown hand, which I reproduce here. Jackie, found it in the family home in Houl Road when clearing the house.

Jackie and the author.

WEST SHORE
Ladysmith Well; Probably Rossies well to begin with.
Adams Well; Farther down Mayburn.
Hughsons Well; At gable of house.
Lords Well; Eart kent.

HOULL

Houll Well; In nort toon.
Meadow Well; At foot of nort toon.
Giffords Well; In Giffords park.
Scottfield Well.
Spoot Well; Below Kirk, fed from Scottfield.
Trows Well; In park be-aest Kirk, the blocking up of which is said to have brought a melishen on said park. Laekly fulishness.

MID SHORE

Lamas Well; On east side of burn and not far from north dike of Frazer park. There was a gate in east dike opposite well which I was told when I asked Archie Bews about it that it was there for the convenience of the public, and Mr L F U Garriock did not dare to build it up.

Jeannies Burn, as it was called in my young days was also used for drinking and cooking.

There was also a built well in front of Walter Scots shop at the top of the brae about where the little concrete dyke joined the iron railing. There was a pump on it when I remember it first.

EAST VOE

There was a well near Caty Stane, and Jeannie Yorston's Well further south, and another in the little Quarry benorth Castle Garden and one in the nor-east corner of the quarry, across the road about where Pirga had his stable. I think there was one in front of Duncans house at one time. In fact there is enough good water in this valley to wash Scalloway off the stead if it was properly tapped.

There is also two or three wells on Berry. One in Dicks burn, Houll, and one in front of Turnbull's door, one at Utnabrake, one in the east meadow of Upper Scalloway. One in the west meadow and Ingaville is nearly afloat so why they had to go all the way to Njugal's water with a pipe for is more that I can see through. I have forgot the well in Jeannies muddow. When I was a boy at Gibbleston there wis a pipe taken up the park from that same spring and the water from it could rise to the aeshin heads of the Ha and dere is also da Castle well an meby more if folk kent whaar ta look.

SKIRTS

Whin I wis young an coortin.
A while fae syyne, you ken,
Mony's da nicht we sat aboot
In a peerie but an ben.

Mony a story wis telt
An mony wis da rankle,
Bit aa o da lasses legs you saa
Wis a peep aboot da ankle.

Aboot da time we mairret
In nineteen forty tree,
Hems wir hentit up a bit
Til just below da knee.

An as da years wore on,
Da hems dey got still higher,
Dan da men hed something tae look at
As da weemin drew closer tae da fire.

An shun wir lasses twa
Sat smoking bi da lum,
An da bits o skirts dey wore
Wir just below da bum.

Fashions noo ir changed again
An I tink at somehoo ir idder,
Wi skirts swingin waa doon below da knee,
Dir gittin just lik dir midder.

LOST

The sky is dark
The light is gone
I wander I know not where.
The sounds of night are all around,
I am lost.

A sheep coughs
A night bird calls
See them, no I cannot.
The sea breaks on an invisible shore,
I am lost

I see a light
A door opens
A dog barks, a human voice.
The cliff edge appears, I fall,
I am lost.

Fiction
GLEN

I HAD NEVER been in the habit of visiting my cousin Robbie and his wife Maggie Ann at their remote croft, Runnaness, reached only by boat or a hike over the hill from Runnavoe. I had got to know them more closely while they were on a holiday in Aberdeen. They were staying in a bed and breakfast close to my student digs when I met them in Union Street. Robbie said that he had never walked the length of Union Street without meeting someone from Shetland. It was Maggie Ann who saw me first and we chatted for a while. They invited me to have meals with them, which for a student was just great. I was really sorry to see them go back to Shetland after their holiday and promised to visit them on my vacation.

I phoned them soon after I got home and a visit was arranged. I stayed a weekend at Runnaness and went with Robbie for walks in the hills and round the large loch. Always we were accompanied by Glen, their very friendly sheep dog. Glen was black with a white neck, chest and legs, and had a distinctive bark, like a cough and bark put together. At night he slept beneath the restin chair, which stood along the back wall of the but end of the croft house. In the evening while we sat and talked he lay in front of the fire. He was part of the household, and a member of the family; in fact he was the only family Robbie and Maggie Ann had.

Back in Aberdeen after the summer vacation, June, my Aberdeen girl friend and I decided to get engaged, and at Christmas time she came to Shetland with me for the festive season. I phoned Maggie Ann one night and she insisted we had to visit Runnaness. June was a great hit with Robbie and Maggie Ann, but more so with Glen. He was at her side the whole visit, and his tail wagged all the time. When it was time for us to return to Lerwick, Glen looked so sorrowful that June knelt and hugged him, while we all laughed. Maggie Ann told us that later on that night Glen howled; well, she said, "he greeted".

Time passed, summer came round and once again June and I were on the *St Clair* heading north. I had been promised a job in a fish factory and dad had obtained a job for June in a shop. After a couple of weeks we were to spend a weekend at Runnaness with

Glen. Photo: Clement J. Williamson

Robbie and Maggie Ann. It was fine weather and we really enjoyed ourselves on the croft. As was expected, Glen never left June's side, he was with her all the time. When I appeared in the morning Glen's tail would wag and I would wiggle his ears, but when June appeared his whole body wagged and he made little noises. It was amusing, but very touching. The summer wore on and soon it was time to board the St Clair back to Aberdeen.

One of the men at the factory had asked me if I would like to take part in their squad at Up-Helly-A'. I jumped at the chance, so on the Friday before the big day we landed at Lerwick. I had a lot to learn before Tuesday evening, but June enjoyed the weekend.

Maggie Ann phoned our house and spoke to Dad, "Is yon pair home? Tell them we will expect to see them on Thursday morning."

It was not an invitation it was a command. Monday morning saw snow showers and it was very cold, but Up-Helly-A' morning dawned fine and clear with the temperature just below zero. Lots of people were milling around the town, and in the evening crowds gathered for the procession, which as usual was very impressive and went without a hitch. Afterwards, mam and June went to the Town Hall, dad stayed home, and June said she had danced all night, the two of them only getting home at seven o'clock. It was a great night of feasting, music and dancing, a night to remember. I enjoyed being with the squad boys and June enjoyed the company at the Town Hall.

It snowed a little on Wednesday night and it was a white world we looked out to on Thursday morning. Mam thought we should forget about Runnaness and just phone Maggie Ann, but we were young and full of high spirits so we got a taxi for the ten-mile run to Runnavoe. Leaving the taxi, we set off up the hill. The sky to the north was very dark and ominous and little flakes of snow were starting to fall but there was no wind so I was not really worried. Reaching the top of the hill and looking down the other side, June said, "You can't see anything now for the snow, its getting thicker. There is no sign of the Runnaness house, or the loch. Do you think we will be alright?"

"Of course we will," I replied, but now feeling far from confident. "If we walk down and to our right we should come to the loch, and from there we turn left and we should see the house."

Soon we were at the side of the loch. "Here we are," I said cheerfully. "Now we go left."

GLEN

We walked along the water's edge for a time and I gradually realised I had no idea where we were. Then June said, "The snow seems to be in my face now."

Which way were we heading? Was it north, south, right or left? I had to admit we were lost.

We stood together for a few minutes, then June said, "If we were to shout do you think Robbie might hear us?"

"Always worth a try," I replied, so we both shouted, "Help!" as loudly as we could.

The silence was alarming. Once again we shouted, then June said, "Did you hear a dog?"

I said nothing.

"There it is again. It's Glen, I know that bark. Glen, Glen," she shouted, "we are over here, come boy."

Now I too could hear the bark, that sounded like a cough as well as a bark. There was no mistake, it was Glen all right. What feelings of relief came over us. Glen would soon lead us to the house.

"Look, there he is," June said, as a black form appeared in the now quite heavy fall of snow.

Another bark, and we followed, the black form of Glen leading on ahead of us. We seemed to walk a considerable distance before we bumped into a stone wall. Now I knew where we were, it was the kale yard before the house. We walked alongside the dyke and soon we could make out the porch. Knocking and opening the door we stumbled inside, looking like two snowmen.

Robbie and Maggie Ann appeared and there were handshakes and hugs all round. We divested ourselves of wet snowy clothes and boots and soon were sitting talking while Maggie Ann got the kettle on to boil.

"You were very lucky to find the house in this snowfall." Robbie said. "It's about as heavy a fall of snow as I've seen in many a year. Good job you didn't have this at Up-Helly-A'. Boy, tell us about the squads. Did you enjoy the night?"

So I launched into a tale of what I had seen and June was telling her story as well, and sometimes at the same time as I was. We rambled on for a time while Maggie Ann set the table and soon we were munching away on bannocks and fresh butter.

265

Suddenly June jumped up, "Goodness me, where is Glen? If it hadn't been for Glen we never would have found the house. We were completely lost in the snow, no idea where we were, then we heard Glen barking. He appeared through the snow and led us to the house. Where is he, is he still outside?"

Robbie and Maggie Ann looked at each other, but neither spoke. Robbie got to his feet, went to the cupboard and produced a bottle of whisky and four small glasses. In silence, he poured into each a measure. June was still on her feet looking perplexed. Robbie lifted his glass and said, "Let's drink a toast to Glen, the finest dog that ever was."

We drank, Robbie continued, "You ask where Glen is? Well, I will tell you, his grave is at the south end of the loch. He died in August."

THE BLACK BELT

FIVE LONG YEARS had gone by since I was last in Shetland. I was now home for a holiday and on my way to visit Uncle Geordie and Aunty Maggie, who had a croft halfway along Gallow Voe, south of the huge head of Gallow Ness. Da Ness, as it was called, was flat and green on top, with a large mass of rock overhanging the sea. As bairns we were always warned to stay off the Ness, but bairns will be bairns and we sneaked to the top many a time.

There was no road to Uncle Geordie's croft. It was accessed by a walk of about two miles over the hills. As I crested the hill that day, and looked to where we spent our summer holidays, my mind registered something odd about the scene down below. I stood for a moment in thought, then realised that the whole of Da Ness had gone – vanished into the sea, nothing remaining but a long rocky slope.

I walked on down the hill, across the valley and up towards the croft, where I could see Aunty Maggie out working in the kale yard. She saw me too, and when I got to the house they were both there to greet me. After hugs from Aunty Maggie and much backslapping from Uncle Geordie we went into the house. The but end was just as I remembered it: table at the window; Shetland restin chair along the back wall; upright chair at the side of the fireplace. The open fire brought back memories of childhood days – a much younger Aunty Maggie baking bannocks on a girdle – warm bannocks, which were spread with fresh Shetland butter and greedily devoured by the assembled bairns. No one baked bannocks like Aunty Maggie.

I sat in the restin chair and we exchanged news and spoke about bygone days, and soon it was tea time. The table was soon set, and bannocks, yes Aunty Maggie's bannocks, homemade butter and kirn milk were brought out. When the tea had drawn, we sat in at the table, me facing the fireplace wall. As I looked along the mantelpiece I noticed that the small wooden case which sat there was empty, its glass front removed – the black belt was gone.

Willie's Tales & Travels

As a child visiting the croft for holidays when my grandfather and grandmother were still alive, I had always gazed with wonder at the black belt with its gleaming silver serpent buckle, lying there in the glass-fronted case. No one could touch the belt as the case was glued tightly shut. Furthermore, it was screwed to the mantelpiece. I had often asked about the belt, but was simply told, "It belongs to grandad."

At the other end of the mantelpiece was another case, which housed a model of a full-rigged sailing ship, made by grandad. It, at least, was still there.

After tea, when I was seated again in the restin chair, and Uncle Geordie in the upright chair with his pipe going, and Aunty Maggie was busy with her knitting, I thought it was time to ask about the missing belt. Uncle Geordie stopped puffing, they exchanged a brief glance, and there were a few moments of silence before Uncle Geordie spoke.

"My father," he said, puffing again at his pipe, "brought the black belt home from the West Indies when he was a young man at the sailing. He was a ship's carpenter, and he made the case for the belt. He also made the full rigged ship and its case. He was very reluctant to ever speak about the belt except to say that on no account was it ever to be removed from its case. How he came to be its owner, he never said, but he believed it had evil powers, and should never be handled out of idle curiosity. We all laughed and made light of his fears, but such a man was my father that no one would ever have dared to defy him by disturbing the belt. So the black belt remained in its peat-reek and polish-stained case – that is, until two years ago comes August.

"It was late on a drizzly awkward evening, when a hiker came to the door and asked if we could give him a bed for the night. With the weather being so poor, we could not think to turn him away; so we took him in and told him he could have the bed in the back closet. He talked quite a lot as we sat by the fire that evening. He told us he came from Europe, exactly where in Europe he did not say. His command of the English language was remarkable, and he seemed to be an educated man. Maggie made tea, but never took part in any of the conversation, saying after that he had bad eyes. He seemed fascinated by the black belt. I said, in response to his questioning, that I knew very little about it – only that it was supposed to be unlucky, and should be left alone. However, he was very insistent: 'Could he not take it out of the case to examine it?' he asked. Very firmly I said, 'Most definitely no, not at all,' and changed the subject.

"Next morning, which was bright and sunny, the hiker slept late – it was nearly ten o'clock when he appeared. I was having my mid-morning cup, as by then I had done half a day's work in our kale yard. We conversed a little while Maggie was making his breakfast, and he thanked us profusely for our hospitality, and said that he intended to walk north along the coast towards Hametoon. I then bade him farewell, and went back to my work.

"A while later I saw Maggie set off up the valley. The hiker I could see at the gable of the house, seemingly adjusting his backpack. I was busily repairing the kale yard fence, and some while later, when I looked up I saw the hiker climbing up to the top of Gallow Ness. When he reached the top he turned round, and as he did so a bright flash of sunlight reflected from something shiny about his waist. I never left the house without my eye glass, which I now hurriedly took out and focused on the hiker. A shiver of fear ran through me – I was looking at the silver serpent buckle of the black belt. The feeling of fear turned to intense anger. After our hospitality to him, a foreigner, how dare he take the black belt – the belt that my father had sealed in its case all those years ago. I was furious and set off towards him. As I hurried I saw him pointing at the noost where our boat, a Shetland model built by father many years ago, was hauled up. I watched with disbelief as, to my horror, the boat moved down the lynns and out of the noost into the sea. Then the European turned towards the open voe. He stretched out his arm again, and the gentle ripples became huge waves as the wind rose like a March gale and rushed screaming in the voe. Lifted by the waves and wind, the boat was hurled and dashed onto the beach, shattering beyond recognition.

"I had now almost reached the Ness, and was struggling hard against the wind, but I'm a tough old guy and used to winter gales. The hiker did not see me at first; I could hear him laughing deliriously, intoxicated by the dreadful power conferred by the arcane object fastened around his middle. I climbed as fast as I could, and boy, I'm telling you, I would surely have done him a mischief, but before I could reach the flat green he turned and saw me. As he lifted his arm to point I dropped to the ground. I felt a powerful squall of wind rush over me, and now everything seemed lost; no mortal could fight against this demonic power. In blind desperation I started to speak to the black belt. My exact words I can't remember, but they went something like this: 'Black belt, you have lain in our peaceful home for over 70 years. Do something for me now – get rid of this evil man who wears you.'

"There was a fearful, thunder-like crash followed by a long, echoing rumble. Then everything was still; not a sound, not a bird cry, nor a breath of wind. Face down, I lay and waited, but there was only the gentle swish of the sea along the shore. When I ventured to raise my head, I was looking down a slope of broken rocks. Da Ness had vanished into the sea taking with it and burying under tons of rock, the hiker and my father's black belt.

"I slowly got to my feet and looked around, my legs shaking so much that I could hardly stand. I cast my gaze down the rocky slope and out over the water, but there was nothing to be seen, nothing but rocks and sea. I turned and headed downhill, hardly able to believe what I had witnessed. I came back to the house, put the kettle on the crook, poured myself a dram and wished that Maggie were there.

"When Maggie came home I told her the strange story, and after a long discussion we agreed that it would be best if we said little of the events which had taken place. The next day, I walked over the hill to the post office and reported that the Gallow Ness had slipped into the sea. I also said that a foreign hiker had stayed overnight, and the last we had seen of him was heading for da Ness, on his way to Hametoon.

"About a week later, two men from Hametoon working lobster creels picked up a backpack which they gave to the police, who came and asked questions and searched the shoreline. The hiker was reported missing, and that, my boy, was the end of it. Only the three of us know this story."

Aunty Maggie looked up. "He had bad eyes. It's all best forgotten."

Men and Women of Scalloway who served in the Army, Royal Air Force and Royal Navy during the war 1939 to 1945. Apologies if I have missed anyone.

| Bertie Burgess | Tom Burgess | Willie Burgess | Angus Craig | John Christie |

| Davie Gilbertson | Jimmy Hall | Sidney Hall | Tammie Hall | George Horne |

| Willie Hughson | Willie Isbister | Tom Laurenson | Francis Leask | Jim Leask |

| Sammy Leask | Sonny Mouatt | Tyndall Robertson | Anna Ross | Davie Slater |

Gracie Smith	 Jim Smith	 John Smith	 Lollie Smith	 John Stephen
 Willie Sutherland	 Robert Umphray	 Cecil Watt	 Ian Watt	 Jerry Watt
 Magnus (Ninkie) Watt	 Attie Williamson	 Harry Williamson	 Jackie Williamson	 John Williamson
 Sonny Williamson	 George Wishart	 Jimmy Wishart	 Willie Young	

My thanks for photos go to Zandra Gilfillan, Billy Williamson, Margaret Gronneberg, Tom Laurenson, Nellie Watt, Doreen Halcrow, Jim Smith, Margaret Clark, Arnold Duncan, Nancy Johnson, Jackie Thomson, Mamie Williamson and, of course, Clement J. Williamson.